D1611664

*Music
and Young
Children*

FRANCES WEBBER ARONOFF

New York University

Music and Young Children

HOLT, RINEHART AND WINSTON, INC.

New York   Chicago   San Francisco   Atlanta

Dallas   Montreal   Toronto   London   Sydney

To my mother

The "meaning" of any world depends on the way it is seen, conceptualized, formed. Schoolmen and artists both must organize their experience and make sense of it for themselves. The principle or the mode of organization will vary with temperament, capacity, style of life, and end in view. Some will seek out man's condition under the sky; others will visualize men in relationship, making their laws, achieving their practical goals. Some will see darkness overtaking the light; others will find it sensible only to work in the day. Some will deal in presentations, in efforts to make people feel and form; others will work with fact and truth, informing, making people know. And, at any given moment of history, the "reality" which is defined is in some sense equivalent to the multiple ways in which experience has been formed.

MAXINE GREENE,

*The Public School and
the Private Vision.*

PREFACE

Young children naturally tune in to the sounds of music. They often manifest their spontaneity in body movement. With objectives and processes clarified, music for young children can be a means of combined intellectual and emotional growth, learning that is significant as well as joyful, and far-reaching in its influence. For this purpose the classroom teacher needs to understand the true nature of music as esthetic experience. He must be familiar with the basic concepts involving the elements of music. He must understand the authentic connection of music and movement and, also, the young child's ways of knowing, especially in nonverbal modes.

The esthetic experience of music is dual: *perception* encourages *response*. *Perception*, the cognitive aspect, focuses on the elements—rhythm, agogics, melody, tone quality, dynamics, design, and texture—and their interrelation. The young child may acquire concepts of these elements by listening, moving, singing, playing, and creating, with listening indispensable for the other skills. Affective *response* includes the intuitions and insights into human feelings that the interplay of sound and motion can bring forth. Positive affective response is more likely to occur when classroom experiences are evolved from the young child's life space.

Eurythmics as developed by Émile Jaques-Dalcroze (1865–1950) is based on the time-space-energy relationship of body movement. Its value in learning is corroborated by recent research on preverbal learning. The teacher can build on this research by organizing music experiences according to three ways of knowing as defined by Jerome Bruner. These ways are *enactive*, through action and manipulation, *iconic*, through perceptual organization and imagery (aural, kinesthetic, and visual) and *symbolic*, through words and other symbols. In music-movement activities, the focus is on the interaction between and translation of the *enactive* and *iconic* ways of knowing. The teacher who understands the connection between music and body movement can encourage the child to use his body as a "musical instrument" for physical experience of the interplay of the elements in the musical flow.

The usual unstructured experiential background of young children requires that the teacher be especially flexible in planning learning episodes. Specific directions for him to follow are frequently inappropriate and inadequate. The rationale described in Part One of this book can provide some bases for the teacher's choices. Part Two suggests a variety of music learning strategies. It contains checklists, examples of experiences and evaluative procedures. An appendix defines Dalcroze Eurythmics in the context of contemporary educational philosophy.

I am deeply grateful to those who helped in the first forming of this book: Gladys Tipton, for her expert guidance and for her confidence in me; Sam Ball, for friendly and illuminating dialogues about learning and thinking; Reba Joresh, for her enthusiastic and untiring help in the classroom and for her assistance in recording the children's comments; Adele Davidson, Early Childhood Coordinator, District I, and the teacher-students of New York Public Schools In-Service Course D503, for valuable insights into the classroom teacher's challenge. I thank my friends—students and colleagues—whose reading, listening, and commenting improved the final product.

Most of all, I thank my sons, Don and Bart, for their challenging criticisms of my work. They helped me to question convention and habit, to begin to find my own meaning of what education is all about. Within this framework, this book is addressed to present and future teachers of young children and to music and curriculum specialists. It should also interest educators at other levels and in other disciplines because, in articulating practical music learning objectives and procedures, it indicates the role of music in the total curriculum. Further, the approach it advocates may be a model for learning in other areas, inside and outside of the school. The objectives are specific, but the cues come from the child. The physical-emotional-intellectual interaction facilitates the child's total involvement. It helps him to form a conceptual structure within which he can be open to experience, intrigued by discovery, and motivated to realize his highest potential of intellectual and emotional development.

New York
March 1969

FRANCES WEBBER ARONOFF

CONTENTS

PART TWO

Guiding Experiences in Sound and Movement

Appendix

PART ONE

Formulating Music Objectives

I

INTRODUCTION

Recent research in child development stresses the importance of the youngster's early experience in his total intellectual development. Granting that certain factors are innate, intelligence is now seen primarily as a result rather than as a precondition of environmental stimulation; the child's emotional development is a result, also, of his opportunities to perceive, to manipulate, and to interact with people and objects. Studies of young children, especially of two "special" groups—the culturally-deprived and the gifted—have emphasized the importance of the nonverbal modes of cognition, and they have demonstrated that the cognitive (intellectual) and affective (emotional) aspects of the child's growth are tightly intertwined.

This focus on early childhood has quite naturally caused reexamination of nursery school and kindergarten teaching materials and methods. However, attention to the rationale and means of music and movement activities has generally been insufficient. Music activities for young children have traditionally been concerned with affective development, but they have usually lacked clear learning objectives in the cognitive area. Movement to songs and recordings has been encouraged, but only the superficial relation of body movement to music seems to have been understood.

Thoughtful questioning of traditional activities is in order. What benefits can be derived from nursery rhymes and holiday songs, with and without children's body action? What are the comparative values of movement patterns and "creative rhythms"? What general and musical objectives can be achieved with records especially designed for marching, skipping, and so on? Are other materials and strategies needed?

AUTHORITIES MENTIONED in the text, followed by dates, refer to books or periodicals listed in the Bibliography.

When pressed for their rationale for music-movement activities, teachers typically speak of the need for children to release energy after sitting quietly. (Emphasis on physical activity *per se* can cause neglect, rather than recognition and direction, of concomitant learning.) We constantly hear that music provides the means for self-expression. (The opportunity for the child to express himself can be negligible in traditional activities; it happens only when the predetermined repertoire of music and movement coincides with his feelings or attitudes at the time.) Especially with the recent focus on cognitive development, the use of music in language development has been highlighted; children improve in perception and comprehension and, as a result, in following directions. (Children do indeed learn quickly and well in the non-threatening atmosphere of the music activity, but these "nonmusical" benefits can be greatly increased with more purposive planning for musical growth.)

Because the fundamental experience of music is in fact nonverbal, and because of new insights into the nature of intelligence, a more comprehensive rationale for music-movement activities in early childhood is needed. The potentials of interrelated cognitive and affective growth through the discipline of music cannot be ignored. The child is learning *all the time!* He can be helped to discover ways of generating his own meanings from experiences planned with this objective. It is not enough that he learn the words of the songs and acquire the skill to sing them; he must go beyond learning and use this material to realize and express his feelings. Success in finding his own meanings is possible when the child is directly involved with the elements of music in ways that are appropriate to his experience and development and flexible in their productive use in the classroom. Music through movement can be an important part of curricula for young children. It affords a variety of opportunities for integrating cognitive and affective growth because, by its very nature, it involves perception and participation and the accompanying feelings of the perceiver-participant.

In order to implement a comprehensive program of music, including the necessary emphasis on the cognitive aspect, the teacher needs more than directions of what to do and how to do it. He must understand the dual nature of music and its use as a means of intellectual and emotional development in the total curriculum. If he realizes how the child learns through action and through the organization of his perceptions, the teacher can more easily plan experiences in body movement and listening through which the basic structure of music is accessible to the young child. With process and objectives clearly in mind, the teacher can develop activities suitable to the child's background and environment, allowing the child to organize his perceptions into concepts of music, to acquire basic skills in singing and playing, and to develop positive attitudes toward music perception and participation. Often the spontaneity and confidence generated by self-expression through music and movement is transferred to other learning challenges in the classroom.

THE YOUNGER CHILD
GOES TO SCHOOL

Psychologists today generally agree that all children are capable and often desirous of learning much more, much sooner, than has previously been thought possible. Comprehensive documentation for such views is provided by the examination and interpretation of a large mass of data from hundreds of longitudinal studies on the shaping of human behavior from infancy to adulthood. Regarding the crucial nature of the first few years of life, available data show that "in terms of intelligence measures at age 17, about 50 percent of the development takes place between conception and age 4, about 30 percent between ages 4 and 8, and about 20 percent between ages 8 and 17."[1] Correlated data on the development of general learning suggests that since "about 17 percent of the growth takes place between the ages of 4 and 6, we would hypothesize that nursery school and kindergarten [experiences] could have far-reaching consequences on the child's learning pattern."[2]

On the basis of such data, Millie Almy describes the shift of interest to the intellectual aspects of development. She foresees the challenge to early childhood education as being at least as great, perhaps greater,

[1] Benjamin S. Bloom, *Stability and Change in Human Characteristics*, New York: John Wiley and Sons, 1964, p. 88.
[2] Bloom, p. 110.

than for any other level of education, for it is during these early years that "children acquire and learn to process basic information that can either further or impede their later progress, that may indeed either enhance or stultify their intellectual powers."[3]

J. McV. Hunt states the same view in even more pragmatic terms: "It might be feasible to discover ways to govern the encounters that children have with their environments, especially during the early days of their development, to achieve a substantially faster rate of intellectual development and a substantially higher intellectual capacity."[4]

These theories are being implemented by the establishment of pre-kindergartens for the culturally deprived in many urban areas. The emphasis on early cognitive growth in an empathic, supportive atmosphere is as applicable to music learning as it is to perceptions and perceptual organization in other areas. (The resurgence of the Montessori method, with its emphasis on early motor, sensory and language education, is significant. However, procedures for music education described in the Montessori literature are limited by their reference to a narrow repertoire which is unsuited to our culture and by the requirement of special equipment.)

But Almy warns that many teachers pay only lip service to the emphasis on the cognitive; it is easy to use psychological jargon.[5] Teachers must have a comprehensive knowledge of the subjects they teach, but they must also realize the importance of understanding the ways children think. It is not enough to recognize and label certain stages of growth, with general indications of what is possible at each level; teachers must make every effort to understand the processes of intellectual growth, and seek out ways of using it to advantage. It is not enough to know that young children can be taught to move and sing and play, and that they thrive on these activities and accomplishments; we must identify the conditions for transfer of preverbal understandings, provide for the acquisition of needed skills and musical repertoire, and devise teaching strategies to help children develop heuristic techniques for further cognitive and affective growth in music.

[3] Millie Almy, "New Views on Intellectual Development in Early Childhood Education," *Intellectual Development: Another Look*, Papers from the ASCD Eighth Curriculum Research Institute, Washington: The Association, 1964, p. 13.

[4] Joseph McV. Hunt, *Intelligence and Experience*, New York: Ronald Press, 1961, p. 363.

[5] Almy, p. 12.

THE MODES OF
INTELLECTUAL DEVELOPMENT

To understand intellectual growth, many developmental psychologists turn to Jean Piaget for his comprehensive theoretical and empirical contributions to the study of the child's knowledge at various stages of his development. From these data, which deal with the stages and sequence of a continuous process, Piaget discovered what has been called "the implicit logical theory on which the child proceeds in dealing with intellectual tasks."[6] Bruner praises the utility and power of Piaget's descriptive work but explains that this formal description is not in any sense an explanation or a psychological description of cognitive development. Piaget's descriptive clarity, rather, poses the question for anybody who would deal with psychological explanation. Bruner deals with such a psychological explanation and has clarified the processes of intellectual growth for the nonpsychologist.[7]

As a background for Bruner's ideas of the different ways of knowing, the conventional usage of *intelligence* should be noted. The common conception of this word has often been at least implicitly connected with symbolic representations of experience, whereas most precisely considered the term concerns the capacity for knowledge and understanding (especially as applied to the handling of novel situations) and the capacity for the higher forms of thought. We have commonly tended to consider as *intelligence* only those operations easily tested and analyzed in verbal terms. Preverbal experiences were hazily clumped together and labeled *prelearning*.

Bruner identifies three modes of learning—ways of processing and representing information from the environment: (1) the *enactive*, through action and manipulation; (2) the *iconic*, through perceptual organization and imagery—aural, kinesthetic and visual; and (3) the *symbolic*, through words and other symbols.[8] Recognition of three

[6] Jerome S. Bruner, *Toward a Theory of Instruction,* Cambridge, Mass.: Belknap Press of Harvard University Press, 1966, p. 7.

[7] Jerome S. Bruner, "The Course of Cognitive Growth," *American Psychologist,* 19, 1–15, January 1964; "Theorems for a Theory of Instruction," Jerome S. Bruner, ed., *Learning about Learning,* OE-12019. Cooperative Research Monograph No. 15, Washington, U.S. Office of Education, 1966, pp. 196–211; "Preface," "Cognitive Growth: I," "Cognitive Growth: II," "An Overview," Jerome S. Bruner and others, *Studies in Cognitive Growth,* New York: John Wiley and Sons, 1966, pp. vi–xv, 1–67, 319–326.

[8] Jerome S. Bruner, "The Course of Cognitive Growth," *American Psychologist,* 19, 2, January, 1964.

modes of cognition rather than one, the *symbolic,* places the preverbal aspects of intelligence in perspective. They assume stature not only as ways of knowing accessible to the child before he has language skills, but also as means of substantiating symbolic systems in later learning.

The *enactive* and *iconic* modes of cognition are the very ways in which a young child knows music! We have intuitively emphasized these aspects of his experience, but until now we have perhaps failed to realize fully the musical learning that can take place in these ways. These ways of knowing are the heart of the musical experience. The admonitions of sensitive music educators from Jaques-Dalcroze to Mursell to Lanfer[9]—to *do* and *hear* before finding a symbol for—focus on the *enactive* and *iconic* modes of cognitive growth in music. The emphasis on these modes and the translation from one to the other form the principles of the Dalcroze[10] approach to music education.

AFFECTIVE DEVELOPMENT
IN CONTEXT

Until recently, the young child's early school experiences were especially concerned with social and emotional attitudes, on the supposition that positive feelings about learning were prerequisites for receptivity of content; programs emphasized the establishment of acceptable classroom behavior habits, with secondary attention given to content. The recent work of Bruner and other psychologists, both developmental and educational, is perhaps responsible for the shift away from pre-learning experiences *per se.*

It cannot be overemphasized that education is a dual process: its concern is for affective together with cognitive growth. Ideas are not normally isolated from emotional context by the young child unless or until the child has been taught, directly or indirectly, to ignore or subdue his emotions as he concentrates on the accumulation of knowledge and concepts. He relates his cognitive and affective behaviors in musical expression, especially as he involves his whole body and his

[9] Helen Lanfer teaches improvisation and composition, with raw sounds and classroom instruments, to adults and children in the Creative Arts program at Adelphi University, Long Island, and at the Hebrew Arts School for Music and Dance in New York City.

[10] Émile Jaques-Dalcroze, Swiss composer and music educator, 1865–1950. See Appendix.

personal feelings of previous and current experiences. It is difficult to imagine learning episodes more immediately helpful than an individual's organization of the aural and kinesthetic images he has experienced (what he has heard and what he has felt with his muscles) in conjunction with his physical enactment of the movement of sounds.

Emphasis on cognitive development need not preclude wholesome affective growth; each aspect of growth nurtures the other. Educators must guide the young child's cognitive growth with an everpresent consideration of his attitudes. Music experiences for young children can be planned on a cognitive basis and at the same time easily provide affective benefits; the child's involvement in his own movement and imagery will necessarily cause affective responses.

Thus we need not wait for the child to be "ready" to learn. Readiness can be taught, or at least nurtured; it consists of the mastery of simple skills that in turn prepare the child for more complicated ones. The teacher who is aware of the hierarchy of skills and concepts in music, and of the child's stage of advancement, can plan classroom experiences with confidence and purpose. For example, the teacher will be sure that the child can control his voice and can use it with pleasure before asking him to improvise a musical conversation; the teacher will provide a variety of body movement experiences before challenging the child to perform a "different" pattern for others to follow.

From the beginning of his school experiences it is possible to directly involve the child with significant ideas that will form a broad and stable base for future learning in sound and movement. He can begin to form concepts *of* and *about* music that will serve as the base for his cognitive-affective musical growth. Such a procedure can supply the intrinsic activation for continuing intellectual endeavors.

STRUCTURE IN EARLY CHILDHOOD EDUCATION

In 1956, Philip Phenix proposed that scholars identify the key concepts in each discipline and use these concepts as the foundation for understanding these areas of knowledge. Bruner popularized the importance of planning for this kind of structure in his report of the Woods Hole Conference of 1959. The participants at the conference agreed that the learning of basic concepts and their interrelations form the most pragmatic foundation for the broadening and deepening of knowledge in any discipline, permitting greater comprehension, better memory, more adequate transfer, and continuity through the years of formal and informal education.

McLuhan's work (specifically *Understanding Media*) reflects a similar philosophy. Ours is an age of information overload; there is already too much to learn, and knowledge is expanding at computer speed. Concentration on detail can be frustrating and impractical. The directive is clear; the emphasis in teaching should be on the form, structure, gestalt, and process of the subject.

Kenneth Wann and his associates (1962), in researching the intellectual development of young children, documented the feasibility of pursuing this approach at the preschool level. They rejected the limitations Piaget put on the young child's thinking—that the child begins to be "logical" only at seven or eight. They discarded the concomitant assumption that the intellectual abilities of preschool children extend no further than enumeration and identification. They also put aside the widely held belief that young children are only interested in the "here and now."

The Wann study found that children, some as young as three years, were capable of following through one or more steps of the reasoning process needed for forming concepts, with a concept defined as "a generalized idea or understanding embodying many images and memories which have been blended into a meaningful whole." The acquisition of concepts was viewed as a process of "seeing relationships, categorizing, discriminating, and generalizing about those things which the child sees, hears, and feels in his environment."[11] The emotional component of the process is obvious: the child finds his own meanings in the world around him.

Four researchers have successfully focused on basic concepts in particular disciplines—structure—at the kindergarten level. Spodek's study of Kindergarten Social Science was followed by Robison's in Economics. Subsequently, Fromberg dealt with Science and Blount with Linguistics. In each case, specific experimental work with children was backed by a pragmatic and comprehensive understanding of the behavior of five-year-olds. In the reports of these projects, clear goals in

[11] Kenneth D. Wann, Miriam Selchen Dorn and Elizabeth Ann Liddle, *Fostering Intellectual Development in Young Children*, New York: Teachers College Press, 1962, p. 10.

terms of concepts in the particular disciplines were delineated; they provided purpose and direction for the teacher's planning. Each of these projects provided as well a detailed review of the trends toward using key concepts for planning experiences in the kindergarten.

It should be noted that focus on structure does not necessarily mean isolating the disciplines. In fact, deciding on basic concepts may clarify not only what is unique about a discipline, but also how it fits into the total framework of knowledge. Education is concerned with a larger framework of discipline-structures, made firm by the grammars and processes that are borrowed back and forth, flexible to the changing demands of the social order, even as it helps to bring them about. The classroom teacher has opportunities not available to the specialist to integrate the curriculum.

AVAILABLE MATERIALS
IN MUSIC

Music activities have traditionally been a part of nursery and kindergarten procedures. In addition to using music for tension release and social growth, many teachers have recognized the obvious value of songs and finger plays toward language development. Recently, in this regard, prescriptive techniques for language development through music activities have been provided by several teams working with disadvantaged children. However, the *musical* emphasis in the suggested procedures is superficial, and no music learning objectives have been defined by these specialists. In the literature not focused on special groups, neither of the most recent books concerned with intellectual development and curriculum planning in early childhood education considers music as a discipline, structured or unstructured.

But the idea of structure is not new in the field of music education. In 1948, Mursell advocated planning for musical growth: "Musical growth, like all mental growth, is a process in which essential meanings are clarified, deepened, and broadened."[12] The developmental approach he advocated focuses on the essence of the discipline so that the beginner's experience can be similar to the professional's in quality, although obviously not in degree.

[12] James L. Mursell, *Education for Musical Growth*, Boston, Mass.: Ginn, 1948, p. 50.

Mursell's views on guided growth in music, summarized a decade later strongly refuted the associationist psychology of learning popular at the time. He argued instead that the purposeful treatment of significant musical experiences—listening, moving, playing, and singing—would result in increased musicality.[13] It is easy to see the direct connection between Mursell's "multiapproach" and Bruner's "modes of cognitive growth," between Mursell's cyclical development and Bruner's spiral curriculum.

The ideas of Mursell and of Bruner are illustrated in the standard school music series. In the various kindergarten books, the authors describe the behavioral characteristics of young children, and include lists or charts of musical concepts to be developed. Adeline McCall includes these features geared for nursery schoolers as well. Along with the songs there are suggestions, with varying amounts of detail, for music learning and "creative" experiences in singing, playing, listening, moving and dramatizing the songs. (See the Bibliography.) Correlated poetry is provided, as well as piano selections and recordings for parallel listening.

THE TEACHER'S CHALLENGE

To use this material with purpose, the teacher must establish his own rationale to guide his planning: he must give some thought to what music is, and how it functions as human expression; he must explore and understand the nonsymbolic ways of knowing accessible to the young child; and he must clarify his teaching strategies in the light of these. With such a cognitive framework he can more effectively help each child to discover a structure that will give meaning and value to his creative experiences as it provides the foundation for his musical growth.

---

[13] See also, "The development of musicality is the primary aim of music education from kindergarten through twelfth grade." *Music in Our Schools: A Search for Improvement* (The Yale Report), OE-33033, Bulletin No. 28, Washington, U.S. Government Printing Office, 1964, p. 6.

II

BASES FOR THE YOUNG CHILD'S MUSIC EDUCATION

Specific directions for procedures are inadequate for the preschool teacher; he must be especially flexible when he works with children whose experiential backgrounds are limited or unstructured. If his teaching is to have focus, his flexibility must find support in a basic philosophy, not only in terms of general educational goals for the children, but also in terms of the discipline he is teaching.

If the teacher can eliminate the prejudices and stereotyped conceptions of what music is and what it is not, he can examine its true nature. He can deal intellectually with form in the broadest sense—the disciplined interplay of the musical elements—and he can recognize the intuitions and insights into human feelings that this interplay of sound and motion can bring forth. The teacher can effectively guide the children toward esthetic experiences if he realizes fully that such experiences have two aspects—perception and response. The repeated references in the literature on esthetics and education[1] to the functional similarity between the artist and the child underline the connection between art in all media and growth—intellectual and emotional. This connection in turn focuses on the importance of expert guidance in musical experiences during the early years.

THE SEARCH FOR A PHILOSOPHY OF MUSIC EDUCATION

The authority for a basic rationale for music education at any level would logically be the music specialist. However, an integrative phi-

[1] Rudolf Arnheim, "Expression," Morris Philipson, ed., *Aesthetics Today,* Meridan Book, Cleveland: World Publishing, 1961, p. 198; Kornei Chukovsky, *From Two to Five,* tr. and ed. by Miriam Morton, Berkeley, Calif.: University of California Press, 1966; Harold Taylor, "Music as a Source of Knowledge," *Music Educators Journal,* **51,** 36, September–October 1964.

losophy is yet to be formed by music educators, although increasing numbers realize the need for such a philosophy to "serve as a source of insight into the total music program and . . . assist music teachers in determining what the musical enterprise is all about, what it is trying to accomplish and how it should operate."[2] Charles Leonhard has been an outstanding figure in these discussions, synthesizing the contributions of educational philosophers and summarizing the possibilities and limitations of their help. Without minimizing the contributions of the educators and psychologists, Leonhard suggests that our beliefs about music and music education may be more directly validated by esthetic theory.

This approach to the problem was systematically pursued by Robert Clifford Smith at the University of Illinois. He sought a basis for the rationale for music education in various esthetic theories, in turn derived from certain "world hypotheses." Smith described four general esthetic systems and attempted to apply them to music education. He implied that one of these should be "right" for music, and that music educators must choose among the systems. The fact that the hypotheses are mutually exclusive, however, suggests that each informed person must choose in large measure on the basis of extra- or nonmusical criteria. Smith started with general esthetic theories and tried to fit music education practices into them. On this basis, his categories were inappropriate and, for the most part, irrelevant.

Smith's project concluded with a more practical though less philosophic suggestion than the one with which it began—that music educators discuss their immediate and practical problems among themselves and try to solve them, meanwhile trying to clarify their beliefs with the continuing study of esthetic theory. Both Smith and Leonhard seem to think that discussions among music educators about their problems will lead to the clarification of their beliefs and principles.

But the broad directive for music educators to study esthetic theory is fraught with difficulties. The music education enterprise operates at many different levels; it is guided by specialists with highly divergent training and ideals. Moreover, if the limited time the specialist can

[2] Charles Leonhard, "The Philosophy of Music Education, Present and Future," *Comprehensive Musicianship*, Washington, D.C.: Music Educators National Conference, 1965, p. 42.

spend with children is to be of real value, the classroom teacher must follow through with purposeful activities. Especially in the years before the first grade, the classroom teacher often must initiate and implement the program himself. In either case, it is he who must have a solid rationale for music learning.

THE NATURE OF MUSIC

Let us begin with the basic ideas of the nature of music itself, the simplest esthetic theory of music in layman's terms. The focus will be on the fundamental notions about music that have been verified by recent psychological research—behavioral and educational. A clear explanation of the nature of music, the musicians' basic beliefs, can serve as a guide for classroom use. Such an explanation should also clarify the place of music in the educational enterprise. (Admittedly there are complicated problems at more advanced levels of the music education enterprise to challenge the specialists. Relating psychological, philosophical, and more involved esthetic theories to these problems is undoubtedly helpful. However, their application to practices will perhaps be most useful if the nature of music itself remains the basic issue.)

The history of music begins with the history of man, for man has always organized sounds in time, more or less purposefully. Music accompanies group work and play, including dance, pacing and unifying the physical efforts involved. It amplifies and extends poetry and drama in many settings, from the love song and the lullaby to the miracle play and chant of worship. Thus, for many thousands of years, music has been used in everyday living and it has been combined with other art forms.

As music began to evolve as an independent art form, increasing numbers of musicians and philosophers "explained" it as an expression of human feelings; the esthetic bases of their explanations were naturalistic, symbolistic, or metaphysical. The basically opposite position taken by Hanslick in 1850 against the champions of these views was a significant contribution to modern thought in the esthetics of music. Jack Sacher has translated Hanslick's famous definition of music as "forms moving tonally." He interprets Hanslick as saying that "music should be in some way analogous to the 'dynamic' of feeling, 'the basic relationship of tension and release.' "[3]

While there was a time when some musicians were interested solely in the interrelationship of the structural and stylistic elements (perhaps because of their concern in establishing music as an independent art form) most musicians of today acknowledge the potential affective response inherent in the manipulation of musical materials. In this regard, the consensus of contemporary musicians has been summarized by Bennett Reimer in 1964[4]: "The formal or syntactical content of music is . . . isomorphic with, or analogous to, or reminiscent of, or capable of giving rise to intuitions of or insights into, some very deep and basic facets of life and reality." This statement is corroborated by the formalists more general definition of a work of art, visual or literary as well as musical. They define a work by its formal properties, which have the capacity not only to *order* but to signify, to carry "meaning," to serve as signs.

The most characteristic quality of the making of a work of art is the intense interaction between the artist and his materials. The composer is controlled by his medium almost as much as he controls it. This interplay is what makes the process of esthetic creation unique among human activities. The voice and the body are the most direct instruments with which man expresses his feelings. Sound and motion are the composer's materials; he develops and refines, shapes and forms them, embodying his own deeply subjective insights in the relationships between them.

Thus, music is not only an experience of the composer; the performer and the listener participate in the esthetic experience, which may be described as the sensitive apprehension of the work. The performer is in a sense the composer's collaborator, recreating the primary shaping of the musical materials. He is challenged with interpreting and projecting the composition. The (true) listener actively participates in the musical experience, albeit less directly. He responds and shares in the work of the composer through the medium of the performance.

[3] Jack Sacher, ed., *Music A to Z,* Based on the work of Rudolf Stephan, New York; Grosset and Dunlap, 1963, pp. 57–61.
[4] Bennett Reimer, "Information Theory and the Analysis of Musical Meaning," *Council for Research in Music Education Bulletin,* 2:17, Winter, 1964.

This relationship of the composer, performer, and listener is ideal. But the insights into the "very deep and basic facets of life and reality" that the composer has woven into his materials are only potentially available. The potential is realized to the extent that the listener is able (1) to perceive the system of interactive events in a given composition; and (2) to respond affectively to the tensions and relaxations which are generated by the interplay of events.[5] These are respectively the cognitive and affective aspects of the musical (esthetic) experience.

As the teacher realizes that music, to be music, must operate in both of these areas, he can convey this to the child in an elementary way. The opportunity to respond physically to contrasting sounds of simple instruments, to *high* and *low, long* and *short, fast* and *slow*—to experience the flow of the music with his body—encourages the child's sensitive response as he begins to form musical concepts.

COGNITIVE-AFFECTIVE ASPECTS
OF THE YOUNG CHILD'S GROWTH

It is significant that this interrelationship of feeling and thought that characterizes the esthetic experience is as well the focus of contemporary educational thought. It has become clear that the child needs both cognitive and emotional abilities to function effectively in the school environment, and outside of it. It is the school's challenge to foster the interaction of the child's thought and feeling, one disciplining the other, to help him to find his own way of dealing with his environment.

The esthetic aspect of learning becomes crucial to education when education is thus clearly defined as the process of cognitive and affective growth toward the goals of intelletual and emotional maturity. Music has tremendous potential in this regard, especially because of its availability to very young children in forms that they can use and understand. Teachers who have not understood the cognitive learning potential in preverbal experiences have limited their goals in large part to the affective area. Superficial accomplishment in early childhood music has often been the result.

[5] Bennett Reimer, "The Development of Aesthetic Sensitivity," *Music Educators Journal,* 51, 34, January 1965.

The prime concern of music experiences in the classroom is to nurture, develop, refine, and deepen the child's perception of music; his increased awareness of music's structural and stylistic elements will nurture his responses to it. How can these objectives be accomplished?

Focusing on the importance of structure in musical growth, we should survey the objectives and emphases of music study at various levels and in professional as well as general education. From such a study, Reimer has brought three approaches into focus. The first is the development of factual knowledge and *concepts about music*—"what art is supposed to do and what it is not supposed to do; what kinds of things should happen to one in the experience of art; how artists create; what the various [other] arts are made of and how their materials work; the historical and social context of particular art-works."[6] These considerations were previously only the concerns of the musicologist, the esthetician.

The second method is analysis—studying *concepts of music*. Here we deal directly with the materials of particular music. The purpose of analysis is to improve the individual's perception of the music by recognizing the particular use of the elements and how they are put together.

The third method is performance; it includes *skills and repertoire*. The skills are various ways of manipulating the materials of music. *Listening* is the most important skill; it is essential to *singing, playing, moving,* and later, *reading* and *writing* of music. Repertoire, in addition to music previously composed, includes improvisation and composition, either of which can be as simple as a two-tone chant.

For a viable music curriculum all three of these approaches must be used, and integrated, from the very beginning of music experiences— even in prekindergarten and nursery school. This conviction is supported by the recent research of intellectual development in early childhood (see Chapter I) and by the experience of the author and of other teachers following this approach. Bruner wrote in 1960 that any subject could be taught effectively in some intellectually honest form at any stage of any child's development. His 1966 version of this hypothesis

[6] Bennett Reimer, "The Development of Aesthetic Sensitivity," *Music Educators Journal,* 51, 35, January 1965.

is significant in that it focuses on the young child's preverbal ways of knowing. As the child forms concepts of music through guided manipulation of the elements of music he may begin to develop skills in listening, moving, singing, playing, and creating. As he acquires a repertoire of musical sounds and songs, he can discover his own feelings toward his perceptions.

The discipline of music includes *concepts of music, skills and knowledge* for applying them, and *concepts about music* dealing with the uses of music in the past and on-going culture. Their interrelationship is in fact the *structure* of music. The very young child can be ready to accept all of the approaches to music from the beginning if the material is appropriately presented. In fact, his perception and comprehension will probably be facilitated, for the methods complement each other. The approaches can strengthen and clarify each other for the teacher as well as for the child—or even more for the teacher because his broader background of knowledge affords him more opportunities for seeing and making imaginative relationships.

THE CHILD—THE ARTIST

Viewed in this way, the structure is also the framework within which freedom is possible—freedom for the young child to explore and to discover his world and himself, to become aware of his feelings and thoughts, and to develop confidence in his decisions. This freedom to respond with feeling is easy to nurture in the young child because perception in the early years is characterized, in part, by these significant features: it is *autistic* or subject to the influence of affect, and it is *egocentric* in the sense of having a central reference to the child as observer. It is also *dynamic* in the sense of being closely related to action.[7]

The young child's use of his imagination in free response is explained by Almy: "Not yet understanding which aspects of his environment are likely to remain constant and which will change momentarily, the young child lives, at least for the time, in a world of many possibilities.

[7] Eleanor J. Gibson and Vivian Olum, "Experimental Methods of Studying Perception in Children," P. H. Mussen, ed., *Handbook of Research Methods in Child Development,* New York: Wiley, 1960, pp. 311-373.

Thus, he is often much more inclined to experiment and try than is the older youngster."[8]

The young child's intuition and imagery and his direct representations of his world through action and manipulation seem to be the very ingredients of esthetic expression! Both the child and the artist "find spontaneous excitement in the dynamic, or expressive qualities . . . the most powerful and immediate qualities of the percept."[9] The comment of Ulric Neisser is pertinent: "Some persons see much more than others of the natural shapes and colors about them. The artist's world is filled with shapes and colors that go unnoticed by the less perceptive. He has somehow maintained—and developed!—the integrity of assimilative systems that are absorbed or displaced in the rest of us."[10] *The child's assimilative systems are not yet absorbed or displaced.*

Every person has the potential capacity to respond directly with *enactive* and *iconic* representations, independent of verbal symbols. Harold Taylor suggests, however, that "at its brightest and most responsive, one finds the supreme sensibility in the young child, where as yet the capacity to respond to life has not been dulled or tarnished by a set of imposed verbal symbols in which it is customary to find one's expression. Thus in the young child we find a natural poet, a natural musician, a person who is accustomed to responding to aesthetic values by his very nature."[11]

THE FOCUS OF MUSICAL EXPERIENCES IN PRESCHOOL

The challenge to early childhood education in music is well defined: it must maintain and develop the child's natural responses to esthetic values. In movement and sound experiences, as cognitive learning occurs in nonverbal modes—directly from perception—concepts can evolve from personal experience and discovery. Such a procedure can allow for a variety of "correct" responses, promoting positive affective

[8] Millie Almy, "Wishful Thinking about Children's Thinking?" *Teachers College Record,* 62, 405, February 1961.

[9] Rudolf Arnheim, "Gestalt Psychology and Artistic Form," Lancelot Law Whyte, ed., *Aspects of Form,* Bloomington, Indiana: Indiana University Press, 1961, p. 198.

[10] Ulric Neisser, "Cultural and Cognitive Discontinuity," *Anthropology and Human Behavior,* Washington, D.C.: The Anthropological Society, 1962, p. 69.

[11] Harold Taylor, "Music as a Source of Knowledge," *Music Educators Journal,* 51, 36, September–October 1964.

growth, and using success as a motivating factor. The incumbent freedom to respond (within given limits) will develop the child's imagination, flexibility, and fluency in his musical thinking, and perhaps in his general attitude as well. (Considerable insight into the nature of music can be achieved by experimenting with musical materials, and encouragement to explore is an essential part of learning by discovery. But not to differentiate between such explorations and the work of gifted artists can easily distort the very values we are seeking to nurture.) Through singing and moving and playing, alone and with his classmates, the young child can demonstrate his accomplishments and thereby achieve the human dignity borne of being productive.

If the teacher is thoroughly aware of the genuine musical goals he would pursue, music can permeate the child's school day. Without this awareness the development of authentic musicianship is easily thwarted by superficial experiences. Examples of them are the practices of singing songs with attention to the words only, using recorded "background" music to control the noise level of the classroom, and allowing indiscriminate banging on classroom instruments for tension release. Such practices can only result in desensitizing the child *and* the teacher.

THE STRUCTURE OF MUSIC

The structure of the discipline of music is the framework for planning learning objectives, starting with the youngest children. It consists of two kinds of concepts—concepts *of* music and concepts *about* music—with repertoire and skills as the means of establishing and developing the concepts.

Concepts of Music

Attaining general concepts of music is the (cognitive) process of identifying the attributes that characterize the separate elements of music considered in their simplest form. The pervading goal of planned music experiences is the child's perception of these musical elements.

The concepts should be delineated for the student in such a general way that they can serve as the basis for comprehension, no matter how complicated or how extended future developments in the discipline prove to be. Their definition should evolve from the consideration of a broad range of musical materials—from sixth century plainsong to contemporary compositions of all types.

The element of melody includes chromatic (and even glissando) as well as diatonic motion in the context of atonal as well as various tonal relationships. (Avoiding melodic clichés may in fact help to focus on the intervallic motion—the shape of the melody.) The general concept of prose, as against metered, rhythm should be noted: freely shifting rhythmic patterns may follow speech, as in Gregorian chant, or evolve from movement explorations in space. Meter can be five or seven as well as two, three, or four. In conceptualizing texture, tones sounded together should show a variety of tensional thrusts. Open fifths and the most dissonant intervals, as well as relationships derived from triadic harmony, should be exploited in many contrasts of registers.

The classifications of the elements as listed here are somewhat arbitrary, for there is constant interplay and overlap; no element of music operates alone. The comments are those of prekindergartners, near the end of a year of purposive experiences. Some were spontaneous; others were elicited by such questions (after a particular experience) as "What did you hear?" "What happened in the music?" or "How did your feet [arms] know what to do?" Many children who responded accurately in movement and singing were not necessarily interested or able to describe their actions or perceptions.

RHYTHM

1. *Beat*

"When you listen, you can keep clapping or walking to the music, and it feels right."[12]

2. *Even sounds equalling less than a beat*

"You can run or tap faster than before, and it still feels right."

3. *Accent*

"When you're walking or clapping, some steps or claps want to be harder."

[12] Reba Joresh and Frances Aronoff, Anecdotal records of music sessions conducted by the writer, October 1966–June 1967, Pre-Kindergarten Sections 1 and 3, P. S. 134M, New York Public School, 40 Montgomery Street, New York City.

4. *Meter*

"A big swing fits the music, too."

5. *Shape*

"*Long's* and *short's* mixed."

6. *Patterns*

"*Long's* and *short's* mixed; you can do it again the same way."

7. *Rests*

"Little places have no sound; you stop and listen for what comes next; you have to be ready."

8. *Prose rhythm*

"Some sounds are longer because their words need more time."

"Some last longer because it takes more space to play them."

"You don't feel like clapping or anything; you just feel like listening to the shape of it."

AGOGICS

1. *Tempo*

"The *fast* or *slow* of the music."

2. *Changing rate*

"It got faster, little by little."

"It got slower, little by little."

MELODY

1. *Pitch*

"The *low* or *high* of the sound."

2. *Direction*

"The music is going *up*."

"Now it's going *down*."

"It is staying on a *level*."

3. *Shape*

"You can tell a song by the way it goes up and down."

"Sometimes you can tell a song without the up and down, when somebody just claps the way it is."

TONE QUALITY

1. Voices

"Every person sounds different; when you close your eyes you can tell who it is."
"You can talk and you can sing."
"You can sing words or 'la-la' or 'ooooo.' "
"You can hum and you can whistle."
"You can make things sound smooth or jerky."

2. Raw sounds

"You can clap lots of ways that sound different, with both your hands or on different parts of yourself."
"Hiss; buzz; cluck your tongue; snap your fingers."
"Tap a wine glass with a fork."
"Tap the table [floor, shelf] with a pencil."
"Some people can make a sound blowing over the top of a bottle; some can blow through their teeth."

3. *Nonpitched percussion:* rhythm sticks; wood block; different sizes of drums; tambourine; jingle bells; triangle; cymbals
4. *Pitched percussion:* melody bells; piano
5. *Stringed instruments:* violin; guitar
6. *Wind instruments*: recorder; clarinet; trombone

DYNAMICS

1. Soft and loud

"The music is soft, gentle."
"The music is loud, strong."

2. Changing

"The music is getting louder, little by little."
"The singing is softer and softer."

3. Accent

"It's a surprise, all in one place."

DESIGN

1. *Repetition*

   "The same way over again."

2. *Contrast*

   "A different sounding part."

TEXTURE

1. *Single line*

   "One person is singing."
   "One thing is playing."

2. *Combinations*

   "Everybody is singing the same song."
   "Everybody is playing the jingle bells the same way."
   "He is singing and clapping [playing] the song at the same time."
   "You can sing a song and play the drum where the words aren't; then you can hear all the words."
   "The piano is 'singing' the song—the teacher is doing it—and her other hand is playing other sounds to go with it."

Repertoire and Skills

As the child listens, considering and concentrating on one aspect of a musical experience, he is building a repertoire of songs, and of patterns and qualities of sound. (He sometimes learns the label for a concept before he understands the concept completely; then he may use the term as an aid in organizing his perceptions.) The more he hears, the richer will be his rewards during subsequent learning episodes; he is constantly gathering material as he develops musical skills.

The musical skills have been traditionally delineated as listening, moving, playing, singing, creating, and later, reading. Careful consideration of this list reveals that all of the skills do not operate at the same level. Listening must be involved in all the other skills. Similarly, creating is on a different level from the others because it cannot be done in isolation, that is, it must have a medium—moving, playing, or singing.

Concepts about Music

Concepts about music are intimately involved in the child's esthetic response, his appreciation. As he becomes more cognizant of the interplay of musical elements in the total sound, he begins to understand them and to evaluate his reactions in a very elementary way. Leading questions and comments from the teacher can focus on the esthetic, historical, and social aspects of music in general and the classroom repertoire in particular. The resultant discussion complements the child's personal engagement with music in the classroom.

What is music?

"Nice sounds."[13]

"Singing songs we like."

"Making nice sounds together."

"Singing how you feel."

"The sounds from the record-player."

"Records when you play them."

Who makes music?

"Children."

"Teachers."

"Mothers."

"Fathers."

"Birds."

"Everybody."

"Singers and people who play the guitar on TV."

"People who play together to make a record."

Why do people make music?

"For playing games."

"For working together."

"For marching: children or soldiers in a parade."

"To help babies go to sleep."

"For telling, in a special way, that you love somebody."

"It's a good way to tell stories."

"It reminds you of different ways you feel: happy; scary; funny; like resting."

"Because it sounds nice, and you want to hear what will happen next."

[13] Reba Joresh and Frances Aronoff, music sessions October 1966–June 1967.

Where do people make music?

> "In school; at home; at the playground."
>
> "On TV and the radio."
>
> "Sometimes at work."
>
> "Around a camp-fire—Indians."
>
> "At a round-up—cowboys."
>
> "At church."
>
> "At a party, to dance."
>
> "At a concert."

How do people make music?

> "Sing; hum; whistle—you don't need words."
>
> "Clapping and tapping."
>
> "Playing on a piano, drum, violin, etc."
>
> "You can sing [play] by yourself, with your friends, or in a big orchestra."

Who makes up music? (Discuss, and subsequently label, folk and individually-composed music.)

How does the music [a particular piece] make you feel? (Give children the opportunity of describing their peers' physical interpretations —their facial expressions and their body movements.)

How do you [or teacher or person in an orchestra] learn a particular piece?

> "By listening to the teacher or another grown-up sing it."
>
> "Hearing a record over and over."
>
> "Remembering nice shapes of sounds you make yourself."
>
> "Sometimes the words help you remember."
>
> "Knowing how to read music."
>
> "Learning how to play the piano, recorder, etc."

SUMMARY

The bases for the young child's musical education are found within the interpretation of education as the process of cognitive and affective growth toward the goals of intellectual and emotional maturity. To plan for such growth in music the teacher should understand the structure of music—that it includes both perception and response, as in any esthetic experience.

The structure of music, consisting of concepts *of* and *about* music and the acquisition of skills and repertoire, is the framework for planning music-learning objectives. In this regard, the similarities in the intuitive and direct responses of the artist and of the young child are significant. They indicate the challenge—to maintain and develop the child's natural responses to musical (esthetic) values.

III

THE PROCESSES OF MUSICAL GROWTH

The general concepts[1] of music are the functional supports for musical growth. Once they are defined, prescriptive techniques for achieving them must be planned. But there are still many unknowns in the processes through which the child actually sees relationships, categorizes, discriminates, and generalizes. A practical approach is for the teacher to choose a particular hypothesis from the consensus of broad beliefs of the experts in psychology and education, and to use the hypothesis as a working model. Considerations that may determine his choice will be the nature of the discipline he will teach and the level and characteristics of his students.

Possibly Bruner's approach to the ways of knowing most satisfactorily meets these requirements for early childhood music. Knowing by movement and by perception of aural images are in fact the basis of musical expression. These ways accommodate the development of musical skills and growth in the affective domain as well. When a child feels and acts on a piece of music, it comes to belong to him: he finds his own meaning in it. An added advantage is the verification of Bruner's hypothesis in the successful pedagogical practices of Jaques-Dalcroze and others using his approach. (See Appendix: "The Eurythmics of Émile Jaques-Dalcroze." Kodaly and Orff are among many music educators who acknowledge their debt to Jaques-Dalcroze.) The work done by Dalcroze demonstrates many practical musical applications of the theory that may guide the teacher in planning classroom music experiences for young children.

[1] The concepts that form the structure of a discipline are in reality *principles*—"chains of concepts"—according to Gagne. Robert M. Gagne, *The Conditions of Learning,* New York: Holt, Rinehart and Winston, 1966, p. 141. Carroll retains the label *concept* but indicates that a concept may have a number of relevant attributes. John B. Carroll, "Words, Meanings and Concepts," *Harvard Educational Review,* 34:184, Spring, 1964. This book follows Carroll's usage. The teacher of young children must check for comprehension of the single attributes as a part of the learning episodes he plans.

CONCEPTS AND THEIR ACQUISITION

In large measure, a person understands and can deal with his environment by discovering equivalence in the things around him. The discovery enables him to form concepts, tools that help him function by creating order in his world. A concept is best treated as a hypothetical construct to explain observed facts. A person's possession of a concept cannot be directly observed; but it can sometimes be inferred from observation of his behavior.

John Carroll (1964) calls concepts "properties of organismic experience," with experience broadly defined as any internal or perceptual response to stimulation. There are two necessary conditions for the formation of a concept. (1) The child must have a series of experiences that are in (at least) one way similar. These are positive instances of the concept. (2) Before, between, or after the series he must also perceive examples of what the concept is *not*. For instance, to teach *high* as a concept in pitch, examples of *low* must somewhere be included.

It should be noted that the child can have a concept without verbalizing it; he shows he has it by his consistent physical response to a certain class of stimuli. One who recognizes the *long-short* rhythmic pattern, for example, will gallop or skip the pattern in a listening game that features *long-short* in contrast to even notes of various values, or when it recurs (repeatedly) in a new song.

Some concepts *about* music evolve accidentally from pleasurable music experiences. But the child's affective response can be appreciably broadened by focusing on his sensitivity to the sounds he makes and hears and to the body movements he learns to control. Relating music to learning in other areas of the curriculum is positively indicated as well.

MUSICAL REPERTOIRE AND SKILLS

As the concepts are functional supports, musical repertoire and skills are the building materials of the structure of music. The child needs a repertoire of songs and instrumental compositions or improvisations which exploit various tone qualities, pitches, intensities, and durations. He needs many opportunities to experience these phenomena in the same and in different ways. Experience has shown that the more related his physical experiences are to the sounds of the songs and instrumental selections he sings and hears, the more likely will be his success in organizing them into concepts.

Skills in performing operations (manipulating the materials) may often be the learner's key to comprehending concepts. As he learns to control his movements and to change them at will, the child can feel the consequences of his decisions, and begin to generalize his experiences. He crosses over from learning to thinking.

The line of demarcation between knowledge (of musical materials) and skills is very difficult to draw in music experiences. Musical skills may be designated as listening, moving, singing, playing, and creating, with listening crucial to the others. As the child improves in these skills, he is likely to refine his perception of details in the music. Conversely, his repertoire of songs and musical materials will be the basis of his more skillful moving, playing, singing, creating, and above all, listening.

A combination of teaching-learning strategies is indicated for achieving the objectives of concepts, repertoire and skills in early childhood music. Of these strategies, discovery has been very popular in recent years. (Bruner's writings on the subject have been a strong influence.) Especially in music education it has been advocated for two reasons: (1) to lead to the formation of concepts and (2) to encourage improvising and composing. The association of the discovery method with the recent emphasis on "creativity" in the classroom has perhaps intimidated some teachers. But children imitate the movements of the teacher and their peers, and they learn to sing songs by rote. However, these are but preparations for more useful (transferable) learning. Thus, skills can be taught by imitation, and information stored by rote memory without apology if the teacher recognizes these important and necessary preparations for the development of concepts and for the evaluation of their attainment.[2] It is when the child organizes these skills and knowledge (his experiences of performance) into concepts that he can go beyond them—that he has the means for personal expression.

[2] For a comprehensive evaluation of learning by discovery, see David P. Ausubel, "Some Psychological and Educational Limitations of Learning by Discovery," *The Arithmetic Teacher,* 11:290–302, May 1964; Bernard Z. Friedlander, "A Psychologist's Second Thoughts on Concepts, Curiosity, and Discovery in Teaching and Learning," *Harvard Educational Review,* 35:18–28, Winter 1965; Jerome Kagan, "Personality and the Learning Process," *Daedalus: Creativity and Learning,* 94:553–563, Summer 1965.

A pragmatic connection must be made between the theories of how children learn and the practical applications of these theories in the classroom. Bruner's hypothesis of the three ways in which a person deals with experiences can be a helpful working model. Using it as a guide, the teacher can plan music experiences that are both appropriate for the "autistic, egocentric" young child and intrinsic to the content and qualities of music.

Bruner explains that if benefit is to be derived from contact with recurrent regularities in one's environment, experiences must be represented in some way; simply having them is not sufficient. To be available for use when needed, experiences must be coded and processed for easy retrieval. Bruner (1964) calls the end product of such a system of coding and processing a "representation."

The *enactive* mode is a means of direct representation through an appropriate motor response. Minimum reflection is involved. The simplest musical example is the representation of an even beat by walking, or by the recurrent swinging of another part of the body. No imagery or words are needed for this experience of the beat. This way of knowing might be called "knowing with one's muscles" or "knowing with one's feelings." ("Feeling" could mean through the senses or through the emotions as well as the senses.)

In the *iconic* mode, what the child has seen or heard or experienced through movement becomes transformed into mental images that stand for events as pictures do. These images—visual, aural, or kinesthetic—become his "storage system," which corresponds to the environment. The child is increasingly able to separate what is internal to his own experience from what is external in the sense that it is being shared by others. As he develops techniques for filling in, completing, and extrapolating from his stored model of the world, he becomes able to go beyond the information encountered on a single occasion. Not only can he recall rhythmic patterns and muscular tensions, he can supply new sequences of these representations.

The child's motor experiences and his practice of them seem to be necessary for developing a simultaneous image to represent the sequence of acts involved. In the same way, his repeated movement responses—walking, running, galloping—can be organized in terms of the music that accurately accompanies these *enactive* representations.

Using *symbolic* representation, the child can say to himself or to others what he has done, or what he will do. With words or other symbols, he can go far beyond what can be done with acts or images. He can go beyond the experience of the moment, using longer sequences of events. He can give or take directions for performing in a particular way. In a music activity, he may notate his improvisations, at first perhaps with his own devised symbols, later in conventional score. By experimenting with the symbols, he can even "turn reality over on its beam ends!"[3] engaging in a kind of "creative doodling." As he learns to translate from symbols to sounds, the music of other times and places becomes available to him.

INTERACTION OF THE REPRESENTATIONS

Although the three modes of knowing—by doing, by imaging and by symbolizing—are parallel in the sense that they can be pursued independently, it is the interaction and translation of them that helps the child to learn. In the beginning stages of teaching any discipline "the task of instruction involves some optimal orchestration of the three systems of representing that knowledge."[4] *The planning of musical experiences that make possible such interaction and translation seems to be a crucial strategy in sponsoring the achievement of music concepts interrelated in a useful structure.* Music, by its very nature, focuses on perception and perceptual organization of sound, so the *iconic* mode (with aural images) will be consistently involved.

Studying the modes of knowing separately is a valuable procedure for the understanding of the whole process of learning, but there is some question as to whether the modes can actually be separated so sharply.[5] The connection between body movement and heard rhythm has been assumed intuitively by music educators for some time. This interaction and translation of the *enactive* and *iconic* (aural) modes, and

[3] Jerome S. Bruner, *Toward a Theory of Instruction*, Cambridge, Belknap Press of Harvard University Press, 1966, p. 11.

[4] Jerome S. Bruner, "Theorems for a Theory of Instruction," Jerome Bruner, ed., *Learning about Learning*, OE-12019, Cooperative Research Monograph No. 15, Washington: U.S. Office of Education, 1966, pp. 202–203.

[5] I. A. Richards argues that even visual images are "full of muscles"; Bruner concedes to this possibility. Jerome S. Bruner and others, *Studies in Cognitive Growth*, New York: John Wiley and Sons, 1966, p. xv.

the subsequent use of the *symbolic* mode have been used widely to study beat, meter, patterns, and phrasing. Jaques-Dalcroze, as he developed his ideas in this area, extended the technique to other elements of music, which are in fact organized and controlled by rhythm. The success of his teaching gives credence to the usefulness of Bruner's hypothesis; further analysis of this connection will be helpful.

RHYTHM AND MOVEMENT

"Rhythm" has many meanings. Two current uses in music can be identified. In the more limited definition, rhythm is an element of music which includes beat and meter (organization of beats), duration and rhythmic pattern (organization of durations). These rhythmic features, with their energy components, can be directly realized in body movement. Mursell's rationale (1937) for studying beat, meter, duration, and patterns through body movement states that since muscular sensations—the controls of body movement—can differ only in duration and intensity, their only means of organization is rhythmic.

In a more inclusive definition, rhythm is "everything pertaining to the temporal quality of the musical sound."[6] In this sense, rhythm organizes and controls all the other elements of music, including rhythm in its more limited sense. Such an inclusive definition approaches the definition of music itself. The eurythmics of Jaques-Dalcroze treats rhythm in this larger sense. Indeed we are concerned with the relation of movement to all the elements of music as they interrelate in time.

MUSIC AND MOVEMENT

Music is a human experience. It is not the physical properties of sound as such, but rather man's relationship with sound. Sessions (1965) calls the connection between physics and music occasional and circumstantial, but not essential. Vareze in a 1966 interview includes *space* as an aspect of music because the production of sound involves disturbance or displacement of the atmosphere. In the expressive context, however, the concern is not for space *per se,* but the human experience of it.

[6] Willi Apel, *Harvard Dictionary of Music*, Cambridge, Mass.: Harvard University Press, 1964, p. 640.

One way of explaining man's relationship with sound is to note that the very act of breathing is also the fundamental tension-release that pervades the expressive qualities of music. (More than the simple balanced beat of inhale-exhale is implied.) A phrase played or sung "without a breath" maintains the tension to the cadence—the moment of release. Dancers amplify this kind of breathing into movements of their bodies and extend them by moving their bodies in space.

In music, these tensions and nuances are products of melody, texture, dynamics, and tone quality as well as, more directly, rhythmic and agogic devices. The rhythmic and agogic devices in turn give form and expressive nuances to the other materials of music. The sounds of music move in dynamic interrelationship. For example, tempo, usually denoting speed, is not one musical characteristic in isolation; it is a product of speed and energy and various subtle nuances of tone quality and attack. Experiencing tempo with the body in locomotion is obviously more helpful in perceiving the musical intent than hearing the one-dimensional ticking of a metronome. An interesting commentary on the body movement aspect of music is found in Ross Lee Finney's (1959) description of the movement and gesture that inspire his composition.

The sentient human is capable of using his own body movements for musical expression. Sessions expresses it well: "Music is significant for us as human beings principally because it embodies movement of a specifically human type that goes to the roots of our being and takes shape in the inner gestures which embody our deepest and most intimate responses."[7]

DALCROZE PRINCIPLES: ENACTIVE AND ICONIC MODES

It was from a similar philosophy that Jaques-Dalcroze evolved an approach to music education at the turn of the century. Inspired by the principles of the movement-music relationship, his objectives were achieved through activities based on *enactive* and *iconic* (aural) representations and their interaction. The methods he developed, starting with the individual's simplest movement response to the sounds of

[7] Roger Sessions, *The Musical Experience of Composer, Performer, Listener*, New York: Atheneum, 1965, p. 18.

music, are as useful for developing musical growth today as they were many years ago. Although the classroom teacher cannot be expected to have the rigorous musical training required to become a Dalcroze teacher, there are basic principles that can be adapted and exploited in the cause of effective music education in the classroom.

The child can know a steady beat by walking at his normal pace, using his own recipe of energy and space. His adjustment of the tension and resilience of his muscles and the resultant use of space by his body determine the tempo. Swings initiated in diverse ways, twists, bends, and isolated movements of parts of the body add to his *enactive* ways of knowing tempo, dynamics, and mood.

Music becomes the means of prompting movement,[8] with silence as rest or as punctuation. Sounds having the most distinctive musical qualities (very loud versus very soft, triangle versus rhythm sticks) afford the greatest opportunities for the young child's discrimination in listening and in movement. The teacher takes cues for the music from the child's already demonstrated movement repertoire; he realizes the limitations of the child's natural tempo and dynamic range, and helps him to extend this range. The child responds through his neuro-muscular system, experiencing and distinguishing the pulse out of the flow of the music. He discovers it in himself as he uses his body as his "musical instrument."

As the child hears, he tends to organize his perceptions (*iconic* mode) and to translate these musical experiences into his own movement. He learns to tense and relax at will, and knows the satisfaction of spontaneity and control. Opportunities can be given for him to respond to musical suggestions (follow) and to make independent decisions (lead). (See Chapter V.)

SUMMARY

An effective structure for musical growth relates concepts of the elements of music and concepts about music as human expression. It uses

---

[8] This is *afference*, the excitation of afferent (input) nerves. What operates in the interaction of enactive and iconic modes that follows is called *reafference*. Reafference is a learning phenomenon, defined as "sensory stimulation that is systematically dependent on movements initiated by the sensing animal." Richard Held, "Plasticity in Sensory-Motor Systems," *Scientific American,* 213, 85, November 1965. The phenomenon could be called a motor-sensory feedback loop.

musical skills and repertoire as a means of acquiring these concepts and of giving meaning to their relatedness.

Bruner's ways of knowing provide a working model for planning young children's music experiences that can help to develop such a structure. A crucial feature is the child's interaction and translation between the *enactive* and *iconic* ways of knowing in music-movement activities. The successful work of Émile Jaques-Dalcroze (1865–1950) at many levels of music education gives credence to Bruner's hypothesis and suggests practical applications of it to early childhood music.

PART TWO

Guiding Experiences
in Sound
and Movement

IV

PLANNING MUSIC EXPERIENCES
FOR YOUNG CHILDREN

Part One of this book has been concerned with the rationale for a preschool music curriculum based on the child's potential for learning through his actions and through organization of his perceptions. The focus of the learning to be achieved has been on the discipline of music —concepts of the elements of music, concepts about music as human expression, the use of skills and repertoire, and how all of these are related.

The classroom teacher may need some guidance in implementing such a music program. He may choose between a method—selected materials and directions for presenting them, or a basic philosophy— objectives and processes, and general strategies. The teacher who has had a minimum of music training, or none at all, may reach for the first. A method can indeed provide security for the teacher, but its use has a significant disadvantage: in the preoccupation with set procedures, the teacher is apt to measure his "success" by the knowledge and skills that can be clearly demonstrated by his students; he is apt to lose sight of the long-range goals of musical growth. In this regard the acquisition of concepts, especially in the early years, may well be a function of the planning of learning experiences within the child's life-space. For this reason a method, by definition inflexible, does not lend itself to concept-formation by young children.

On the other hand, the teacher who has firm convictions about the nature of music and the goals of musical growth can find a practical and dependable guide in a simple listing of the elements of music. Within this skeletal structure he can adjust to the individual child's life-space and cognitive style and to the necessary informal environment of the classroom. In this chapter and the next, the concepts guide is supplemented by examples that indicate the responses of one group of

41

four-year-olds. Sample games and diversions are included and teacher concerns are discussed.

CHECKLIST OF MUSICAL CONCEPTS

The classifications used in this outline are arbitrary. Other groupings could be logically made. For example, the items under "agogics" might be incorporated under "rhythm." "Agogics" is used here to separate those aspects not amenable to precise notation.

More accurately, "melody" consists of "motion" (pitch, direction, shape) and "rhythm." However, the term "motion" is not commonly used in this way and is apt to be misleading. Therefore, the concession is made to the general usage of "melody."

RHYTHM

1. Beat
2. Even sounds equalling less than a beat
3. Accent
4. Meter
5. Shape
6. Patterns
7. Rests
8. Prose rhythm

AGOGICS

1. Tempo
2. Changing rate

MELODY

1. Pitch
2. Direction
3. Shape

TONE QUALITY

1. Voices
2. Raw sounds

3. Nonpitched percussion
4. Pitched percussion
5. Stringed instruments
6. Wind instruments

DYNAMICS

1. Soft and loud
2. Changing
3. Accent

DESIGN

1. Repetition
2. Contrast

TEXTURE

1. Single line
2. Combinations

VOCABULARY OF YOUNG CHILDREN'S MOVEMENT

The teacher's awareness of the many possibilities for young children's movement makes it easier for him to encourage their explorations of body movement in space. Especially by using the variations the child can have experience with many exemplars of one concept with a minimum of repertoire learning. Possibilities go far beyond this list: consider combining movements simultaneously as well as enacting two or more different movements in succession, to make patterns.

LOCOMOTION

1. Walk
2. Run
3. Jump
4. Hop
5. Lunge
6. Gallop
7. Skip

NONLOCOMOTION

1. Bend, at all joints
2. Stretch
3. Swing
4. Rock
5. Twist
6. Pull
7. Push
8. Strike
9. Shake
10. Bounce

ALL MOVEMENTS CAN BE VARIED

1. Energy
   a. Levels
   b. Gradual changes
2. Speed
   a. Levels (tempi)
   b. Gradual changes
3. Dimension
4. Level in space
5. Flow
   a. Smooth to jumpy
   b. Sudden to gradual stops
6. Direction: shapes drawn
   a. In the air
   b. On the floor
   c. With the body itself

CLASSROOM INSTRUMENTS:
CHILDREN'S DISCOVERIES
OF THEIR SOUNDS AND USES

Classroom instruments, often called "rhythm instruments" and even "toy instruments," have traditionally been used to form a "rhythm band" or "toy orchestra." There seems little to recommend this kind of activity. Certainly little benefit can be gained from teaching set "orchestrations" to young children, and having everyone "keep time with the music" with all the instruments sounding at once results in a cacophony which can only desensitize the children, to say nothing of the teacher!

But classroom instruments can be used to encourage the discovery of distinctive tone-qualities and their expressive potential as well as to introduce some cause-and-effect science phenomena to the child. They may also present and secure such concepts as pitch, duration, and dynamics. Playing is an opportunity to extend an arm or body movement into sound. As the child experiments with the size and energy of the movement, he provides an immediate feedback of his action. The same kind of experience is possible with clapping, but the sounds produced by good-quality instruments are naturally more satisfying.

Through guided exploration and discussion, the child can acquire skill in controlling the sound as well as the *silence* of the instruments and can gain some understanding of the musical importance of each. Comparisons of tones produced in different ways (by different children or by the teacher) provide instances of concepts dealing with pitch and dynamics. Comparisons of different instruments, singly and in combinations, provide examples of tone qualities and textures.

When children have been encouraged to listen to the unique possibilities of the various instruments, and have acquired the slight skills needed, they can supply appropriate instrumental accompaniments to songs and movements and improvise their own patterns and phrases. (See the section on "Making-Up" later in the chapter.) The following discoveries made by children have been arranged in space to indicate the relationship of their elemental perceptions.

The Voice

A single sound of your voice can be

    low

    high

    somewhere in between

It can be

    loud

    soft

somewhere in between

One sound can

    stop immediately

    last a long time

    keep sounding

        at the same loudness

        at the same softness

    get louder or softer

        little by little

        suddenly

    fade away

Your voice can go up and down to make melody shapes

    in steps

    with wider spaces

    by sliding

It can be smooth

    jerky

Your voice can sing words

    hum

    whistle

    "tra-la" to sound happy

    "oo-oo-oo" to sound sad and lonely

Your voice makes its sounds with the air you breathe and with some special muscles in your throat

Everyone has a voice

Each person's sounds different from everyone else's

Wherever you go your voice goes with you

The Melody Bells

    Each bell has a different sound

        low

        high

        somewhere in between

    You can use more than one to go up and down

        making melody shapes

            in steps

            with wider spaces

                                but no sliding

    The sounds are soft

                  and they   gently   fade   away

    They ring

        they can't be jumpy

    When you hit the metal with the mallet

        it starts to sound

    You can stop the sound by touching the metal

                      but you don't want to

    You can play two bells at the same time

        one mallet in each hand

    Two or more people can play

        at the same time

        one after the other to make a melody

The Triangle

The triangle makes one sound

the sound of a bright bell

The sound can last a long time

It likes time to ring out

The ringing gets softer

and softer

and

softer

For a very exciting ring-ring-ring

put the rod inside the triangle

and hit the three sides

by drawing little circles

as fast as you can

The triangle and the rod are made of metal

You must hold the triangle by the cord

so it will be free to ring

The Tambourine

The tambourine is two instruments in one

a drum

jingles around the edge

you wouldn't think of

trying a melody on it

but it's great for dancing

You can play the jingles without the drum

shake your hand in and out

make any shape with your arm

in space

Play the drum part with

your knee

your elbow

your knuckles

with the tambourine held almost anywhere

the jingles play cheerily along

The Drum

The drum sounds many different ways
almost like talking
depending on how you play it
with a felted stick
with your knuckles
with your fingers
the soft tips
your fingernails gently scratching
in a design
in a straight line
or even on
the metal rim
the wood of the side
It can be
very soft
very loud
all ways in between
The drum booms best when you bounce away from it
as if you are lifting the sound out
Our drum is made of a wood frame and tightly-stretched skin
You can carry it around and play it
as you march
as you do an Indian dance

The Rhythm Sticks

The rhythm sticks make dry clicks
just the moment you play them
no ringing
no singing
no higher
no lower
with not much difference in
loud
soft

The rhythm sticks are fine for keeping the beat
as you sing
as you march
you just tap one with the other
To make a scraping sound
rub one across the notches of the other

If you're sitting down
try them on the floor
make a galloping rhythm by tapping
the stick for the *short*
the floor for the *long*
(one hand does all the playing)

The Piano

Each key on the piano has a different sound

very high

very low

many different in-betweens

Each sound can be

soft

loud

in between

They stop at once

if you take your finger off the key

unless you save them

by putting your foot on the damper pedal

Even if you keep your finger on a key

the sound

fades

away

gradually

So the piano can sound

smooth

jumpy

You can use different fingers to play

as many as ten keys at once

call the bunches

chords

clusters

Play them gently and listen carefully

Is it the kind of sound you want?

Since each key is

    low

    high

    somewhere in between

        you can go

          up

          down

              to make melody shapes

                  in steps

                  with wider spaces

Melodies and chords or clusters can be played together

                  in no end of ways

SOLO MOVEMENT INVENTIONS

Movement inventions are best evolved from classroom situations—recollections of individual or group experiences, or stories read by the teacher. They are useful as a change of pace from concentrated listening or from movement activities that have become undisciplined. The experience of the extremes of tension and relaxation promotes the child's increased control of his movements, giving him confidence to explore new modes of self-expression. Not governed by musical accompaniment, each child establishes his own combination of speed and energy.

Movements that Show

1. Imagine you are full of jumping beans, from the top of your head to the tip of your toes, and even to the ends of your fingers. Let all the beans jump at once.
2. Move one hand back and forth so fast that it makes a breeze on your face.
3. Pull an imaginary rope tied to an imaginary balloon that is very far up in the sky. Let the rope coil up at your feet.
4. Soft, fluffy clouds are falling. Punch them back into the sky.

Movements "Inside You"

1. Puff yourself out as big as a circus tent.
2. Make yourself small enough to rest on the end of a pencil.
3. Make yourself so stiff you can only be moved or lifted in one piece, like a plank of wood.
4. Be as limp as a rag doll. (This is not easy for some people. Test for complete relaxation by lifting an arm or a foot.)

GAMES

Music-movement games for young children have the primary purpose of providing opportunities for practice and improvement of listening skill and muscular control. The children should help to decide on the "rules" of the game, and demonstrate the desired responses. There are no losers because the "contest" is not between children; it is between each child and the particular musical stimulus of the game.

Ordinarily a game should not be used to introduce a concept. Rather a particular concept is presented in a learning sequence through a variety of activities during the course of which its label is provided. However it is often while playing the game that the child discovers the generalization of his responses; he organizes his repeated sound-movement experiences into the concept.

This kind of game provides the ideal opportunity for the teacher to study the child's status in cognitive and affective growth, information essential to his subsequent planning. Each child demonstrates his skills and understandings; he unconsciously "acts out" as well his feelings and his individual style.

Games with Teacher Supplying the Music

elephant

1. *Who Are You?* Giant, bird

Decide to be an Indian chief or an Indian brave. The chiefs walk only when they hear

The braves walk only when they hear a melody, such as

Walk anywhere in our "forest" but do not bump into other Indians.

2. Statues

Follow the music in any way you choose, inventing gestures with your arms, head, and body as you move around the room. When the music stops (without warning) "freeze" into a statue. (Notice the various poses.) When the music starts again, move again, finding new gestures.

3. March or Conduct

If you hear a low melody on the piano, march to it, as if you were part of a parade. If you hear a high melody, stand in one place and move your hands in time to the music. Be ready to do either one. Stand still and listen if there is no sound.

4. Contrary Mary

Move the "wrong" way *on purpose!* Walk when the music says to run. Run when it says to walk.

Games with a Child Leading

1. Follow the Leader

The leader chooses a song to sing and decides how he will move to the music. Everybody sings and follows his movement.

2. Either-Or

The leader's hand-claps tell everyone to walk, but when he walks, everyone must stand still and clap for him.

3. Play What I Play

Everyone except the leader closes his eyes. The leader plays even beats—fast or slow, loud or soft—on the drum, triangle, rhythm sticks, or piano. Everyone pretends to play the same kind of instrument in the same way. Later, try simple rhythmic patterns, changes of dynamics, changes of tempo.

4. Quick Change

The leader plays the drum for everyone to walk. When he changes to taps (on the wooden side of the drum)—without losing a beat—everyone stands still and taps his own shoulders. Each leader may change several times.

"MAKING-UP"

The environment for the concentrated work of improvising and composing may require special planning. Perhaps "making-up" will be a choice activity for a small group. Certainly there should be no coercion to participate.

Experimenting with Orchestration

1. Choose a song; try the following, one at a time.

    a. Play as you march to the song.

    b. Sing the song; play only on the important beats.

    c. Sing the song; play in the empty spaces between the words.

2. Sing the song.

    a. One person plays every beat.

    b. One person plays only the important beats.

    c. One person plays in the empty spaces between the words.

Change instruments and play as in "2." Compare the different combinations of instruments. Can you hear the words? Substitute humming or "la-la's" for the words, or ask the teacher to play the melody on the piano or melody bells.

Patterns of Metric Accents

1. Play individual names on a rhythm instrument.

Repeat without pause, using a beat for each syllable. (Step the beats and count the syllables to be sure.) The others clap only on the strong syllable, the more syllables in the name, the bigger the movement of the clap.

2. *Make patterns by combining two or three names.*

(Do not discourage uneven measures. If someone distorts the even beats in order to have even measures, have the children realize this. Compare the effects and discuss.)

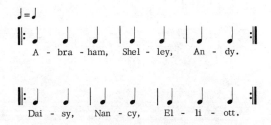

3. *Change instruments and repeat the pattern.*

Which way do you like the best? (Taping facilitates hearing and discussion.)

Patterns of Durations

1. *Playing Your Name.*

    a. Say your name over and over to a slow beat.
    b. Play your name on an instrument as you say it.
    c. Play your name without saying it out loud.

2. *Make patterns with several names.*

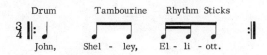

    a. At first, say the names as you play them; later, just "think" them. Each person uses a different instrument.

b. Change instruments and repeat the pattern. Which way do you
like best? (Taping facilitates hearing and discussion.)

Melodic Shapes

1. *"Find" your name on the melody bells.*

Rich - ard   Jen - ni - fer

2. *Make a longer piece using your name.*

Hi,   Rich-ard.   Glad   to   see   you, Rich-ard.

Jen - ni-fer's mer - ri - ly swing-ing with me,

Patterns of Tone Quality and Rhythm

Two or three children playing different instruments, make patterns.
They may decide to have one sound last a longer time, or it may be
played more than once.

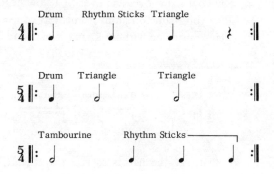

*I Have Had Little Interest in Music in the Past,
and No Training; Where Do I Begin?*[1]

1. Begin by "opening your ears" to the sounds around you. Cultivate the habit of "tuning in" at odd moments, and feature listening as an activity in the classroom. The children's direct and sensitive awareness, when encouraged, cultivates your own openness to experiences.

2. Find sound-producing objects in the environment. Experiment with repetitions and combinations of the sounds to form musical shapes.

3. Tape environmental sounds to play and discuss with the children.

4. Imitate environmental sounds, with your voice and with classroom instruments.

5. Study the ideas about sound as expressed in children's books.

6. Relate these listening experiences to the separate elements of music. Make a conscious effort to isolate the sound from other sensory stimuli. Study the expressive quality of the sound in terms of the interplay of musical elements.

7. Use Gladys and Eleanor Tipton's *Adventures in Music* for Grades 1 through 6 and the *Teacher's Guides* as a basis for self-instruction. Listen to each selection (many times) and study the "Highlights of the Music." They are listed in order of their probable perception, from most obvious to most subtle. Try the suggested responses in movement; experiment with instruments. Study the background information provided about the music and the composer, and explore the examples of poetry and art that are suggested for related experiences.

8. Attend demonstrations and workshops of children's music activities. Evaluate your observations by asking yourself,

    a. What is the objective of the activity—skill, knowledge, or concept? Is it appropriate for the level of the group?

    b. Does the activity provide opportunities for total physical in-

---

[1] The questions are synthesized from discussions with experienced early childhood teachers. In-Service Course D503, Music and Movement Experiences for Young Children, District 1, New York City Public Schools, Fall, 1966.

volvement and perceptual organization? Does it use the learning strategy of translation from one way of knowing to another? Could this work in reverse?

c. What prerequisite concepts are implied?

d. What visual imagery is required of the children? Is it appropriate? Is it helpful to the musical experience?

e. How can I adapt this activity for purposive use with my children?

I Can't Carry a Tune; Is This an Insurmountable Problem?

Everybody can sing! Listen to the ups and downs of your own speaking voice to realize you are not a monotone. If you were told you couldn't sing when you were a child and haven't tried since, you have a problem, but not an insurmountable one.

1. Experiment with talking, noticing your range and then exaggerating the inflections; include exclamations such as "Whee!" "All Aboard!"

2. Imitate sounds in the environment—a truck roaring by, the hiss of the radiator, the clock ticking, the wind howling.

3. Take a few lessons with a good voice teacher to get you started. Then explore on your own.

4. Match your voice tones with the piano.

5. Sing along with recorded songs.

6. *Practice* the material you plan to use with the children.

   a. Experiment to find the best starting pitch.

   b. Use the piano or melody bells for support in the beginning.

   c. Use a recording of the song as a support (not substitute) for your singing. A prerecording (on tape) by a fellow teacher is often preferable to a professional recording, if it is made to your specifications. One young teacher who needed the piano to help her "carry the tune" prerecorded her own materials. Then she had the necessary freedom to move with the children in the classroom.

Must I Be Able to Read Music?

No, but musical "illiteracy" limits you unnecessarily. Reading music, at least enough to understand the examples given in a text and to pick out a melody on an instrument, is not difficult. Study the rudiments from an elementary text or workbook and enjoy exploring at the piano, with song flute or recorder, ukulele or guitar. Formal study in a class will naturally provide commensurate rewards.

Must I Be Able to Play the Piano for Movement?

No, although the piano has potentially a great range of musical effects, making it an ideal instrument for accompanying and stimulating movement. But the piano can also be a hindrance to free movement; unless or until the teacher has the training and experience to improvise musically and fluently, leaving him completely free to attend to the children's responses, he should not depend on the piano for use with movement.

Simple improvisations with the voice and with classroom instruments, however, are very useful. They can be closer to the children's world and they have the added advantage of being available as models for the children's own "making-up" activities—as they lead in music-movement games, and when they begin to join words and music of their own.

Folk and composed songs and portions of instrumental music can be used to supplement and enrich your vocal improvisations. By singing without words ("la" or another neutral syllable), you can capitalize on the expressive potential of your voice as a musical instrument.

Can Records Be Used for Children's Movement?

Yes; they should be carefully chosen for the focus of the experience. The musical effects that are created by a full orchestra playing fine music certainly cannot be approached by a single person in the classroom.

However, experience has proved that the prime requisite of musical stimuli for the movement experiences of the very young child is flexibility, not only in the actual tempo of the music, but in timing its introduction. The child's movement should cue the music, which is possible with improvised singing or playing, but not with a recording. A careful evaluation of data collected by Jersild and Bienstock (1935) documents this limitation.

Of course, children learn to adjust to given music rather quickly, and indeed some very young ones are already adept at it. But some cannot, and understanding the logical process will obviate problems and permit more efficient learning.

In the early experiences, the child's movement should be the activating force of the musical experience: the focus is on the *enactive* representation. After the feedback system (*reafference*) has been established, the process can be reversed to focus on translating the *iconic* representation to the *enactive*. When the child's movement repertoire can easily accommodate a range of dynamic and agogic functions, benefits of the richer musical stimuli (on records) can be more fully realized.

A final word about your freedom to improvise vocally: with it you can be ready to reinforce a child's rhythmic movement during other activities in the classroom and on the playground. If you have as well an extensive repertoire of children's songs, you can permeate and enrich the total prekindergarten program with music learning.

How Much Space Is Needed?

The space for movement activities should be large enough to permit a child to run or gallop freely within it. It should allow each child, standing still, to stretch out in all directions with his arms and legs and not touch anyone.

The most practical plan for locomotion activities may be for everyone to move in the same direction around the available space. Children can be shown how to pass each other to keep the "traffic" moving if the person in front of him is in his way. No emphasis should be placed on "keeping a circle" or "staying in line." Until a child has become confident of his own movement in place, and his movement independently in space, adjustment to the movements of others may inhibit his natural response.

Interestingly enough, a very large area is not recommended. The extra room for freedom of movement can cause difficulties in hearing the music, and in settling down to a cohesive group for singing and discussion.

With the Strong Emphasis on the Child's Freedom to Move, Is Discipline a Problem?

Most children have seemingly boundless stores of energy, especially in bare or stockinged feet and with lots of room; discipline can be a problem, but it need not be. Anyone who has witnessed or played the game of "Musical Chairs" realizes how intently children listen when the music gives the commands. The discipline is inherent in the playing of the game. The same is true of other music-movement activities because the body control is determined by attention to the inanimate sound stimulus. Even a child who may not, for one reason or another, respond to a teacher's request, will rarely disobey a drum! Another time you may give him the opportunity to play the directions for movement.

Some change of activity may be indicated after a period of concentrated listening; there are controlled ways of "letting off steam." (See the section on *"Solo Movement Inventions"* earlier in this chapter.) Discipline is perhaps less of a problem in movement activities to the extent that the activities are suggested by the children and tailored to their needs.

Which Traditional Children's Games Are Suitable for Preschoolers?

The choice will depend very much on your particular group of children. Try the following criteria: Will the children, in playing it, have the opportunity to strengthen a concept or improve a skill? Is its meaning appropriate to their development?

Some people may claim that a game should be "just for fun"—for recreation. This is only partly true; the real fun comes from meeting a challenge. The teacher, as a professional, tailors the challenge to the children.

When playing a game with young children, avoid the traditional directive to "join hands in a circle." The orderly appearance of this activity may be admirable, but the incumbent physical restraints should be noted. The child must walk sideways or twist his body with resulting discomfort; his arms are anything but free to swing. In this position, adjusting to the music is difficult. In addition to his physical discomfort, the child is perhaps not holding hands with his favorite friend, and he wishes he were!

Some Children Are Satisfied to Imitate the Movements of Others; How Can You Encourage Individuality of Response?

1. For a movement in place ask, "Can you do that
   a. "With a different part of you?"
      (Example: clap elbows instead of hands.)

b. "Higher/lower?

c. "Sitting down/standing up?

d. "Reaching backwards/toward the window/toward the door?"

2. For locomotor movements ask, "How would you do that if you were

 a. "A giant?

 b. "A [particular] . . . animal?[2, 3]

 c. "In deep snow?

 d. "In the wading pool?"

3. In action songs ask, "Can you do that

 a. "Louder/softer?

 b. "Bigger/smaller?

 c. "Jerkier/smoother?"

4. Teach songs that feature parts of the body, eliciting appropriate movement.

5. Play "Charades," encouraging exaggerated pantomiming of work movements, actions of machines, representations of natural elements.

6. Experiment with "Shadow Shapes."[4]

How Can You Help a Child Who Doesn't Seem To be Able to Carry a Tune?

Never make an issue of a child's inability to sing, but try to diagnose his problem. Begin by rephrasing your question, "How can I help the child who doesn't carry *my* tune?" The song may be pitched too high (rarely too low) or he may not be hearing it.

Seek out every opportunity to encourage and develop sensitive listening and tone production in every aspect of school experiences. The teacher's freedom to make sounds of all kinds is essential. By example, he can give the child confidence to

1. Imitate environmental sounds, emphasizing extremes of range;

2. Explore speaking voices in dramatic play and story telling (offering a contrasting version in a monotone is effective);

3. Contrast speech and song in participating experiences;

[2] Gladene Hansen Fait and Hollis F. Fait, *We Do as the Animals Do.* Minneapolis, Minn.: T. S. Denison, 1962.

[3] Hans Fischer, *Pitschi,* New York: Harcourt, Brace & World, 1953.

[4] Beatrice Schenk de Regniers, *The Shadow Book,* New York: Harcourt, Brace & World, 1960.

4. Make up chants and sound effects to accompany play and work activities (swinging, seesawing, hammering, sweeping) and dramatic play;

5. Find a reinforcing physical action for a melodic pattern. Extend this technique to action songs.

Let the child supply the stimulus for the echo in tone-matching games; immediately reverse the procedure, using his melodic pattern in his range. Other times, reinforce his singing with your own or with the piano. Encourage him to make up a game in which he can provide the sound stimulus as a chant in his own range.

What Benefits Come from Using Good Recorded Music During Other Activities in the Classroom?

If recorded music is used simply to lower the noise level in the room, there are probably no benefits to the child's sensitivity. If the activity is not related to the music, in effect you are asking him either not to listen, or not to concentrate on the assigned activity. The latter may be in fact indicated in some art activities, when music can set the mood or the rhythmic beat for the activity. Some teachers (and many other adults) have insisted that the use of "background" music to absorb extraneous distracting noises is helpful sometimes, and not necessarily harmful to musical learning. This notion has not been proved or disproved. Some of the same teachers, however, as they clarified music learning objectives and became more involved in purposive music experiences with children, found themselves less inclined to use music in this superficial way.

How Can I Help a Child Who Doesn't Step in Time to the Music? Are Some Preschoolers Not Ready to Do This?

Any child can keep time to music if the tempo cue comes from his own walking pace. He should be given many opportunities to start a movement, and then to accompany himself by clapping or playing on an easily managed instrument. His ability to adjust to a range of tempi develops with his guided discovery of the time-energy-space relationship.

Some teachers involving young children in "creative rhythmic movement" claim that children need not keep time to the music in order to derive benefits from the body movement experience. Children do indeed benefit in physical development, and in freedom and expression of imagination. But far greater benefits come from sensitive perception of the music used. The music itself can be an important stimulus for movement. It can also introduce the element of self-discipline that has important developmental ramifications—with cognitive as well as affective and physical rewards.

PLANNING THE MUSIC-MOVEMENT SESSION

The teacher who understands the dual (cognitive-affective) nature of music and the similar duality of viable educational goals can find many ways of bringing children and music together. Recalling the structure of music as a discipline composed of concepts *of* and concepts *about* music, the teacher can nurture the child's skills and his acquisition of repertoire as means, not ends, of growth.

Musical skills and repertoire firmed by understandings can provide an esthetic dimension to other parts of the school curriculum. Other experiences in turn provide meaningful visual, aural, and kinesthetic imagery as springboards for learning episodes in the daily music-movement session. (Preplanning may be necessary to facilitate the clearing of floor space for the session. Children move best, and without distracting noise, in bare feet. Classroom instruments and other equipment should be readily accessible.) Pictures, stories, and actions of people, nature, and machines—recollections of visual experiences in and out of school—can be motives. The sounds the child has heard in connection with actions are others. His own body movements, in organized and free play, are the source of kinesthetic imagery.

The teacher, having chosen the subject which will initiate the session, can use the checklist of music concepts presented at the beginning of this chapter as a master guide. He should identify which concept(s) are inherent in the songs or improvised material to be used, beginning with the most obvious, and then envisage how these concepts can be represented by the young child's body movements (the *enactive* mode.)

As the child becomes totally involved and music is provided or produced to reinforce this involvement, the experiences need no longer be dependent on the initial visual image, or in fact on any visual image. The vocabulary of movement presented earlier can help the teacher to elicit a variety of kinesthetic experiences; then he and the children can proceed with explorations of music to correlate. With concept formation the objective, the teacher can devise strategies through which the child can translate from the *enactive* to the *iconic,* and from the *iconic* to the *enactive* ways of knowing, and the child can begin to organize his perceptions for future music learning use.

It should be clear that a rigid lesson plan is inappropriate and inadequate to the challenge of beginning where the child is (experientially and physically), encouraging his exploration of movement and images, and yet making these activities purposive. Indeed the teacher must "follow along . . . ahead of the children,"[5] ahead in guiding the dynamic interaction of the session toward the stated goals. Use of the concept checklist can give focus and purpose to procedures typified by flexibility and originality. This guided yet free approach can be an efficient and effective means of helping the child to learn what music is all about and to prepare him to enjoy it, as a composer or performer perhaps, but surely as an eager listener.

---

[5] Alice Miel, "Foreword," Kenneth D. Wann, Miriam Selchen Dorn and Elizabeth Ann Liddle, *Fostering Intellectual Development in Young Children,* New York: Teachers College Press, 1962, p. vii.

V

EXAMPLES OF MUSIC EXPERIENCES

These music learning procedures are sample opportunities for *enactive* and *iconic* experiences that have been tried with prekindergartners, examples of how one group of four-year-olds began to build structures for musical growth.[1] Although they do not constitute a "teaching method" all of the music concepts and many different ways of moving are included in the examples. (See the Checklists in Chapter IV.) The songs (and additional ones) were used in many other ways, providing the children varied opportunities to deal with many exemplars of the concepts, in enactive and iconic representations and in translations from one to the other.

Four general strategies are involved in these translations. (1) A music accompaniment is provided for the child's body movement, which has been recollected from previous experience or introduced by the individual's unaccompanied movement exploration. (2) Given a song or instrumental pattern, the child performs a body movement through which he experiences some aspect of the sound provided. (3) The child identifies the concept that he has experienced in movement, heard, or produced by singing or playing. (4) The child is challenged to produce musical examples of concepts in movement and in sound from descriptions or terms given. For example, "Play or show a high sound, then a low one."

The explanatory remarks and additional suggestions that are included indicate the limitless possibilities for "following along, ahead of the children," for entering into their life-space and being flexible to it.

The main criterion for the selection of a song to be used in the classroom should always be your own enjoyment of it. This enjoyment, often a product of your confidence in performance, is contagious. As

[1] Reba Joresh and Frances Aronoff, Anecdotal Records, Pre-Kindergarten, New York City Public School 134 M, 1966–1967.

you analyze the concepts *of* and *about* music that are exemplified in the song, you can plan for the child's learning and enjoyment through it.

Singing the melody of a song, using *la*'s instead of the words, helps you to focus on its musical value. If you are learning the song from notation, you may have to practice until you achieve a reasonable tempo. Then explore the body movement possibilities yourself. What concepts of the elements can be easily represented in this way? A review of the movement repertoire may indicate others.

Be wary of rejecting a song because the rhythm *looks* complicated. Syncopated patterns are not difficult to learn if the words fit easily to the music, and they usually provide a lively quality to the music. In general, consider whether the words of a song are appropriate to the children's experience, and easy to learn.

Folk songs that have evolved from work or play are usually good choices for music-movement experiences and their brevity is an advantage. (Ballads, because they focus on the story line, may not be as suitable for music learning.) Clumsy English translation of foreign songs are to avoided; if a melody is well-defined and appropriate to your teaching needs, sing it with a neutral syllable, or fit your own (or the children's) words to it.

Foreign language songs—those that use only a few words are the most practical—lead to viable learning about music as human expression as they focus on the moods and uses of the song in other cultures. Nonsense songs are appealing to children and they develop skills in articulation and aural discrimination. Jingles from radio and TV commercials need not be excluded!

Where very specific melodic or rhythmic elements have been featured in the examples that follow, some additional songs from the standard kindergarten texts[2] have been cited. These books are also sources of recordings, music stories, and poetry to use in the classroom.

ORIENTING TO SPACE

T: Teacher; C: Child, Children; ——— Activity.

T: What did you see out of your window this morning?

[2] Texts published by Allyn and Bacon, American Book, Follett, Ginn, Holt, Rinehart and Winston, Prentice-Hall, Silver Burdett, and Summy-Birchard are used. Full citations included in the Bibliography.

C: It snowed.
Everything was white.

T: Where did the snow come from?

C: From the sky.
It covered everything.

T: While we were sleeping, "quiet white . . . softly gently in the secret night. . . ." Can you show how the snowflakes fell "down down without a sound? . . ."[3] (Children begin on tiptoes, with hands held high.) Watch Nancy's snowflakes; they are so light, the wind helps them dance around before they fall on the ground. Show everybody, Nancy. ———— See how quietly and gently they dance. Let's all try it, and find your own private place to rest on the ground.

C: Birds fly the same way.

T: Birds do fly quietly and gently, and then they go to their nests. Look around you, little birds, and each of you find a nest. ———— Remember where your nest is; when you get tired of flying, you'll know where to come to rest. Abraham, show us again how a bird flies. ———— See how he flaps his wings, and sometimes he just glides. Does he ever bump into anything?

C: No.
He's like an airplane pilot.

T: And now let's see if he remembers where his nest is. ———— Did he?

C: Yes.
A pilot has to come down to a special place at the airport.

T: Yes, he does; he knows just where the plane should land. You can be a plane or a bird: fly around quietly and gently. That's fine; you are expert pilots and clever birds! Now, come back to your nest, or your special place on the airfield. ————
(No accompaniment.)
Very good. ———— But do you see any birds in the snow?

C: It's too cold.

T: Where are the birds?

C: They flew to where it is warmer.

T: But you didn't; will you be cold? Is the snow too cold for you?

C: We'll put on lots of clothes.
I wear my red boots.
We have snowsuits.
And mittens.

[3] Alvin Tresselt, *White Snow, Bright Snow*, Illustrated by Roger Duvoisin, New York: Lothrop, Lee and Shepard, 1947, p. 1.

T: And when you're all bundled up, what will you do in the snow?[4] (Children experiment.) Can you guess what Stevie is doing? ———

C: Making footsteps.
Making footprints.

T: Everybody make footprints. Try to find places where no one has stepped before. ——— I see Richard raising his feet straight up, then he puts them gently down so his footprints will be very clear. Can you all do that? ——— Now, can you make long tracks? Can you make long deep lines in the snow? How?

C: You drag your feet. (Demonstrates.)

T: And do you remember how to make a snow angel? ——— You remembered; everybody remembered. Now can you be a little snowball? What happens to a little snowball that is rolled around in the snow?

C: It grows.
It gets bigger and bigger.

T: Then roll and roll. . . .

Acting out real and vicarious experiences in the available space without musical demands is a good starter for movement sessions. You may suggest something as simple as "Show how you walked to school today." "Suppose the sidewalks are very crowded, many people going to work and many children hurrying to school; show how you walk without bumping into anyone."

In other sessions, take your cue from the day's happenings or from class discussions. "Be an Indian going noiselessly back to his tepee after a day of hunting; grown-ups—a barber, nurse, librarian, supermarket checker, and so on, going to work; yourself going to your own apartment; yourself going to your own bed to go to sleep." Later, be a rabbit hopping back to his hutch; a galloping horse returning to his stall in the stable; a giant coming home (lunges); a car parking in its assigned garage space. (See *Vocabulary of Young Children's Movement: Locomotion* in Chapter 4.)

Outward quiet is encouraged if the children know they must be able to hear your signal (a single clap) to return to their self-assigned places. The focus is on controlling one's

---

[4] Ezra Jack Keats, *The Snowy Day,* New York: Viking Press, 1962.

own body, using optimum space and yet avoiding collisions with other children.

Sometimes a child unselfconsciously supplies his own sound effects. His natural coordination of body movement with words or sounds he himself makes ("walk, walk," "hop, hop, hop," "come *back,* come *back,*" as he gallops) is an important preparation for moving in time to a given beat. Individual demonstrations should be encouraged. When the whole class moves again, suggest to each child, "listen to your own sound inside you; it tells you how to move."

Mighty Pretty Motion

Might-y pret-ty mo-tion, too-da-la, too-da-la, too-da-la,

Might-y pret-ty mo-tion, too-da-la, too-da-la-la la-dy.

T: What's a pretty motion? Let's watch John's. ———
   (John raises and lowers his arms.) Yes, John, that's fine.
   Let's all do it as we sing the song. (Adjust to speed of movement.)
   ———

C: I have a pretty motion.
T: Show us, Amy.
C: ——— I'm on the see-saw. (She stands and stoops.)
T: Keep going. Everybody do it. Sing along if you like. ——— Amy went—
C: Up high and down low.
T: *High* and *low.* What part of her?
C: Her whole self.
T: And John?
C: He was high and low.
   Just his arms.
T: What other part of you can be high, then low? (Children experiment, using heads, shoulders, single legs.)
T: Kenny has an interesting way. What part of him is high and low?

C: All of him.
    Not his feet; just the top part of him.
    He's reaching high and low.
T: Yes; everyone do Kenny's motion as we sing.

Notice the deliberate use of *high* and *low* to describe the contrasting positions. Use of these terms for positions in space lead naturally to understanding contrasts of pitch. (See *Listening: High and Low* later in this chapter.) *Up* and *down* are reserved to describe the movement of melody. (See *Ladder Melodies.*)

Children can be encouraged to stand where each can see the others; an approximate circle facilitates a relaxed order of "taking turns" to initiate a movement, with everyone joining in. Your enthusiastic participation, even to the point of exaggerating a child's tentative movement, supports individual efforts. It also helps you to adjust the tempo of the singing to the particular action.

Sometimes a child cannot think of a motion of his own. He stands waiting or, more often, repeats a movement he has just performed. But the objective is to expand the movement repertoire (with the satisfying reinforcement of musical accompaniment), so you must be ready with suggestions: "Everybody does a different motion; what other part of you can bend?" "Tommy shook his hands in front of him; where can you shake yours?" "Can you make different sweeps—in the air?"

Another procedure is to remind a child of a work or play movement he has experienced or seen: "Show what you were doing at the easel this morning." "Elliott, can you paint the ceiling [the floor, the wall] by the door?" "Can you 'paint' the air around your head?" "Who can do that with both hands at once?" Whenever possible, guide the child to bridge over from his visually inspired movement into the realm of total kinesthetic awareness. Give him credit for finding his own way of following your hint: "You found a good way, Andrew. See how he uses his whole arm. Let's all do Andrew's way."

Echoing

T:

If I call your name, sing it back to me. Pe - ter

C:

Pe - ter

T:

A - bra -ham

C:

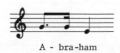

A - bra -ham

T:

Mar - i - sol

(No response.) Let's help Marisol.

C: (Other)

Mar - i - sol

T:

El - li - ott

C: (He half talks, half sings, lowering the pitch.)
T: Perhaps I sang too high for you, Elliott. I'll try again.
     (Approximates range of Elliott's response.)

El - li - ott

C:

El - li - ott

T: Fine, Elliott. (Continues until all are called.) When you answer back just what you hear, I can call you a good *echo*. Everybody can be the echo when I hold out my arms to you. First you listen, then you sing.

La   la   la . . . .

Can you hear me call - ing?   La . . . .

Au - tumn leaves are fall - ing,   La . . . .

Singing the roll call is a good introduction to listening and voice control. Adjust to individual children's ranges where necessary. Casually help those not yet willing or able to sing alone. The rest of the class is usually eager to help! Calling an absent member sometimes causes some child to sing,

He's   not   here.__

You may sing,

What   do   you think   is   the   mat - ter?

to which the child may answer,

I   don't__   know.__

In this way, the simple chant may be extended and gradually a variety of melodic shapes can be introduced and practiced.

To expand your own repertoire for roll-calling in later sessions, borrow fragments from songs that you know, for example:

If   you're   hap - py   and   you   know   it...

If   you're   hap - py   and   you   know   it...

A different kind of roll call gives each child a chance to sing his own name, or "who am I?" with the rest of the class responding. Another is a Round Robin, in which each child calls another, using the same melodic shape, until all are called.

Having a number of motives of the same length—one measure of the same meter—permits more accurate group response, with a minimum of spoken directions. Should some children respond inaccurately, repeat the fragment as the next stimulus, rather than stop the game.

For individual response, the bean-bag game is helpful: the teacher holds the bean bag as he sings, throws it to each child in turn, who echoes and throws it back. The physical action of catching the bean bag sometimes diverts the shy child, helping him to sing unselfconsciously.

The Echo Game can be varied in many ways. The children's responses will indicate their readiness for a new kind of stimulus. For example, occasionally clap one fragment instead of singing it, or try "patsching" (slapping) the thighs, tapping the floor, clucking the tongue, and so on. Provide a series using one of the media, or mix them at will. Eventually *rests* may be introduced by hand movements in space.

Walking; Drum and Triangle

T: When I came into the classroom this morning, I thought I heard a rumbling sound over in the corner. "Who could have come in before me?" I asked myself. "It sounds as if somebody is playing the drum." I walked over to the corner. No one was there. I looked under the tables. No one was there. Just then, I heard the sound again, and it seemed to come right straight from the drum hanging on the peg! (Plays gently on the drum as he says the words.)

I want to be the king. I am the king.

You must do as I say.

C: The king in the story says that.

T: You're right, he does. And then I thought I heard,

Lis - ten   to   the drum,   who   is   king.

Do   what   I   say   to   do,   do   what   I   want you   to,

Lis - ten   to   the drum,   who   is   king.

C: A drum can't talk; you're pretending.
T: Kenny says I'm pretending; what do you think?
C: You are.
    You're making believe.
    You're pretending.
T: You are right; I am pretending. Would you like to pretend with me?
    (General agreement.) Let's say the drum is really the king, and we must
    all do as he says. He may not say any words, but if we listen very care-
    fully, we'll know just what to do. (Teacher plays in tempo of children's
    walk. Several children start to walk. The teacher walks, also, continuing
    to play, reinforcing with free chanting.)

Yes,   yes,   walk   and   walk,   ev - 'ry - bod - y   walk,   walk.

Watch   Shel - ley   walk - ing,   watch   And - y   walk - ing.

(Most of the children stop when the drum does.)
T: You followed the drum's command. I liked the way you walked all over
    our space, and yet you didn't bump anyone. If the drum starts again,
    will you be ready? (Drum beats resume; as soon as all are with the beat,
    it stops. General merriment. The walk and stop periods are of varying
    lengths.)
    Some people are always ready, the moment the drum starts. How do
    you manage that?

C: You have to have your foot ready.
You listen when the drum starts.

T: Do you *not* listen when it isn't playing? Do you close your ears when the drum is not sounding?

C: Your ears can't close!
You can put your hands over them.
You listen all the time, but mostly when it's not playing.
So you can be ready.

T: Yes, you must be ready. You can't take a nap, can you! You have to expect the drum at any moment. Some people call that paying attention.

C: Do you pay money?

T: Not a bit! You just listen! Now I wonder what the drum will do next.

, then stop.
ff

C: It is loud.

T: Don't tell me; show me with yourself. ———
I could tell by looking at you that the drum was loud. Marisol was loud, as the drum was. Do it again, Marisol. ——— Did you notice, she didn't have to make stamping noises with her feet. She felt so strong, she made her hands into fists. Let's all do it that way. (Play fortissimo, starting and stopping. Then introduce pianissimo; children tip-toe. Play as a Quick Response game, varying lengths of walking and stops, loud and soft.)

(Different patterns evolve in subsequent versions of the game; the children step them with appropriate dynamics.)

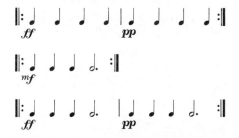

(Each child has a turn giving the commands on the drum.)

T: Yesterday, the drum was king, and we did just as he commanded.

Perhaps a different instrument should give the commands today. What do you think the triangle might want us to do? Listen to its sound. (Plays ♩'s.)

See how the chil - dren are swing - ing and sway - ing.

What made you decide to sway? It looks just right.

C: It's gentle.

Maybe the triangle is a queen.

T: Maybe, but can she be as bossy as the drum? Try it. (Children experiment with swaying and walking tempi, fortissimo and pianissimo.)

C: The triangle can say to walk.

It doesn't sound bossy.

I like the swaying better.

T: Once I saw someone play the triangle this way. (Demonstrates a tremolo: puts the beater in the triangle and describes circles large enough to hit all three sides gently. Some children turn round and round as their fingers "dance" in the air; others roll their hands quickly around each other. These actions are featured in subsequent group response.)

In these songs, the walking beat is sometimes a half-note, sometimes a quarter. It could be an eighth note as well.

Children find many ways to swing or sway to the music, showing the meter by each movement or pair of movements. If you have tried a variety of body movements yourself, with and without music, you will be more able to guide the children's discoveries. Here are some examples to try: (1) Sitting on the floor, arms stretched out, sway from side to side, catching your body weight on alternate hands. (2) Standing, semicircle the arms from shoulder height on one side to shoulder height on the other. (3) With fingertips touching the floor on either side of the feet, semicircle the arms in front of the body to a reaching-up position. If the arms are allowed to swing back past the body at floor level, a helpful knee action can accompany each movement. Encourage optimum use of space. (The knee action serves to extend the child's limits.) If some one does not in fact "go with the music," ask him to show his movement un-accompanied; then adjust the tempo of the singing accordingly.

The triangle is difficult for some young children to manage. Experimentation will bring out the need to play gently and to "watch what you are doing," "keep your eyes on the triangle." Have the children touch the triangle to stop the sound. Experiment, holding the triangle itself and then the holder. Let the children discover that the ringing sound results only when the triangle is free to vibrate.

Finger cymbals are easier to play and provide a similar effect. Show the children how to hold them by the elastics, using the thumb and forefinger of each hand. (Do not wear them on the fingers.) For a clear ringing sound, play the upper edge of one against the lower edge of the other.

You may find a number of household objects that can be "played" for a bell-like, reverberating sound. An aluminum pot-cover, the heavier the better, can be held by the knob and played with a felted stick. (Wrap the end of a rhythm stick or a piece of dowel with felt and fasten it securely.)

Listening: High and Low

T: Yesterday we played the listening game in the park. You heard so many things; do you remember some of them?
C: A truck rumbling past.
The men hammering.
The motor of the crane.
The other man calling directions to the crane man.
The boy whistling.
T: And when you closed your eyes you heard even more.
C: People walking past.
People talking.
Children laughing.
The teacher saying "Sh."

T: I wonder what you could hear in this room. Shall we find out? Close or cover your eyes, and let's be very still. If you hear something, save it until we're ready to talk. I'll say when. ——— Now: what did you hear?

C: The children in the hall.
Miss G said, "Let's go, everybody."
You could hear them walking.

T: Very good. But could you hear anything close—right in this room? Let's try again. ———

C: I heard the clock ticking.
I heard somebody breathing.
Somebody was moving.

T: You're getting better and better! Listen again. Close your eyes; you can listen better. (Plays a low cluster of keys on the piano.)

C: (Immediately.) The piano!

T: How did it sound?

C: Like thunder.

T: Good! I think Yvette remembers what we read in the book about the thick, dark sounds—the *low* sounds of thunder.[5] What else sounds low?

C: A big truck.
A lion roaring.

T: Yes, they make low sounds. How about a cow? Can you make a cow's sound?

C: Moo-oo.
It's a low sound.

T: And a bird?

C: Tweet-tweet.

T: Is that a low sound?

C: No.
It's *high*.

T: How about this? (Plays in high register of piano.)

C: High.

T: And this? (High register again.)

C: That's high.
It's very skinny.

T: Yes; remember the book called a high sound "skinny and tinny."[6] What about this one? (Plays low register key.)

C: That's not skinny and tinny.

[5] Helen Borten *Do You Hear What I Hear?* New York: Abelard-Schuman, 1960.
[6] Borten.

That's not high.
It's low.

T: Good; so the piano can sound low and high. Now, perhaps, instead of telling, you can show whether the sound is high or low. If you close your eyes, your ears work better. (Plays high trills. Some children reach high with their arms.) What did you hear, Debbie—high or low, was it a bird or a lion?

C: A bird.

T: Then it was—

C: High.

T: And how can you show high? ———— Yes; reach up high, be a bird in the air. Now this. (Low register.) Open your eyes and see how Abraham is showing the sound.

C: He is low.
He is a lion who is sleeping.

T: Can you make a high sound with your voice? ———— How about a low one? (Children experiment. Squeaks and grunts are acceptable.) Good. Now, may I play the listening game with you? I will close my eyes so that I can listen very carefully. Rosalind, will you make a high or a low sound for us. We'll keep our eyes closed, and show you what we hear. You must tell us if we are right. (Each child has a turn.)

T: Listen as I sing; when you echo, show the *high*'s and *low*'s with your hand. (Teacher demonstrates at first.)

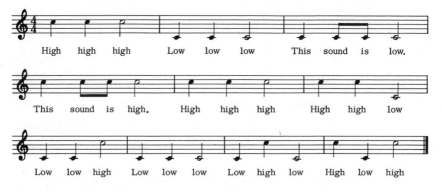

T: What happens when you close your eyes?

C: You listen better.

T: Then close your eyes, and when you echo, this time you may want to show the *high*'s and *low*'s with your hand. (Teacher sings similar patterns of *high*'s and *low*'s—in later episodes with "la.")

Some young children do not like to close their eyes. They may face away from the piano to obviate the use of visible cues (left hand is *low,* right hand is *high.*)

Guard against presenting all examples of *low* as also *loud,* and all examples of *high* as also *soft.* Some four-year-olds have already made this erroneous connection.

Many story favorites of young children provide meaningful examples of *high* and *low. The Three Bears* is a good example; Papa Bear's speaking lines are accompanied with a very low sound on the piano, Baby Bear's with a very high one. Later, Mama Bear's voice sounds in the middle. Individual children are encouraged to identify the likely register for each character and play a sample of the appropriate sound.

In later sessions of exploring at the piano help the child to organize his experiences with the *high-low* concept. Have him choose two sounds; you supply the proper labels— "When this is *low,* this is *high.*" Repeat with other sets of sounds. Give him plenty of opportunities to connect high and low sounds with these labels; do not put him in the position of having to guess which is which. In between times, ask him to identify the sounds you make without his looking at the keyboard. Review the discussion of animal sounds or *The Three Bears* if necessary as you verify his knowledge of the correct labels. (Avoid identifying a single sound as *high;* it will be *low* compared to a higher one!)

Attention can be directed easily to this comparative concept in songs which contain the octave interval. Repeat the passage with the skip, singing with a neutral syllable, having the children sing with you. Elicit labels of *high* and *low* and appropriate body movement—"You show what your voice is singing."

Hiney Matov (Part A)

T: You can echo so well, I wonder if you would like to try an echo song. This song does not use English. It is in another language. Who remembers about other languages?

C: It's how people talk in other places.
People in Puerto Rico speak Spanish.
They speak English in England.
We speak English, too.

T: Yes, we do. And we sing it, too, don't we? But it's easy to sing another language if you listen very carefully. It's especially easy in the first part of this song; you have simply to echo what I sing. This song is in Hebrew. Where do people speak mostly in Hebrew?

C: In Israel.

T: And they sing this song that we're going to sing. It says, "How nice it is to be friends and do things together:"[7]

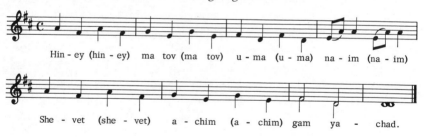

Hin - ey (hin - ey) ma tov (ma tov) u - ma (u - ma) na - im (na - im)

She - vet (she - vet) a - chim (a - chim) gam ya - chad.

T: Since "gam yachad" means "all together," let's really sing that part together. Let's try it. (Indicates descending steps with hand as all sing.) Very good. Can we try the whole thing now, and can you be ready to

[7] Psalm 133: Verse 1 "Behold, how good and how pleasant it is for brethren to dwell together in unity!"

join in for the "gam yachad"? ——— How did you know the "gam yachad" part?

C: You told us.
    You sang it.
    Your hand showed it.

T: How did my hand show it? Can you show that part of the song with your hand? (All show descending steps as they sing.)
    That's fine.
    Would it sound like the song if I sang

C: No!
T: How about this? (As in the song.)
C: Yes!
T: Sing it with me again. ——— Which way did our hands and the song go?
C: Down the steps.
T: And when I sang

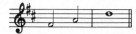

    did it go down?
C: It went up.
T: But the song goes ——— (Demonstrating.) Let's sing the whole thing. Listen for the "gam yachad" and show it with your hand.

> Starting the song on C sharp makes it possible to play "gam ya-chad" on the three black keys. A child who has already discovered the black key groupings on the piano can usually find the descending steps to accompany the last part as the class sings the song. Some children may discover how to play the same relationship starting on another key, or on melody or step bells.

Ladder Melodies

The children have gathered fallen autumn leaves from the park. Most of them are brown. They have cut paper ones of red and yellow after discussing the autumn phenomenon.

T: Where did these leaves come from?
C: From the trees.
T: Did they grow low, near the ground?
C: No, high.
   From way up high.
T: How high can you hold your leaves? Would you like one for each hand, like Elliott? (Teacher sings, holding leaves high; children follow the actions.)

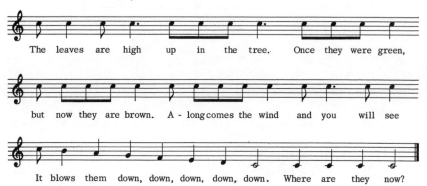

The leaves are high up in the tree. Once they were green, but now they are brown. A - long comes the wind and you will see It blows them down, down, down, down, down. Where are they now?

C: They're on the ground.
   They're low.
T:

This is low when this is high.

Can you put your leaves back on the tree—high on the tree? Let's sing it again. ("The leaves are high" and so on;) ———— (this time add,)

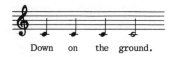

Down on the ground.

How do leaves get on trees?
C: They grow.
   The tree grows and it has green leaves.
T: And what happens in the autumn when the wind blows and the weather is cold?
C: They turn brown.

And red and yellow.
And fall to the ground.

T: And when the spring comes?

C: Other leaves grow out of the branches.
And stay until autumn and then they fall off.

T: Right. Our leaves are on the ground, low. If we want to put them on the "pretend" tree, we lift them—

C: Up.

T:

They're go - ing   up,   up,   up,   up,   up.   Where   are   they   now?

C: Up.
High.

T:

Yes, high.

Shall we do it again? ———

T: Would all the "little Indians" like to go up together? (Teacher crouches

low, with children; all rise a little at a time as Teacher improvises
words.)

All the lit - tle In - dians way down low.. Up they go a lit - tle bit,

watch them go.. Up, up a lit - tle more

al - most there. Look where they are, they're high high high,

You came up with your whole self, with your arms. Can you find a
different way of going up? (Experiment.) See Shelley's way; her hands
are climbing one on top of the other. Let's try it. (All sing ascending
scale with "la.") Can you show the going-up with some other part of
you? Where must that part of you start?

C: Low.
   I did it with my foot.
T: I noticed; show the others. ——— Everyone try as we sing. ———
   I wonder if you can go up and down with both feet! How will you do
   that? (Experiment. There is much jumping.)
   I see lots of up's and down's, but what about the song? Does it fit?
C: You can't sing it fast enough.
T: You are right. Who can find a way of going up *slowly*? (Teacher sits
   down; children sit, too.) What are you trying, Jimmy?
C: If I could stand on my hands, my feet could do it!
T: Yes, but I'm sure you can find an easier way. Let's sing the going-up
   song again, and you follow it with your feet. (Children discover how
   to lean back on their hands.)
   You found a way!
C: Let's do it again.
T: This time let's sing the going-down song. Where will you begin?
C: High. (They sing "We're going down down down down down.")
T: See how Andy is doing it—lying down; then he can get his feet all the
   way up. Shall we try that? ——— While you're up there, would you
   like to take a ride on an upside-down bike? (Teacher holds a child's
   feet and helps him pedal. All sing "There are two little wheels a-turning
   in the air . . .," then the Chorus of *Old Joe Clarke*.

C: I went shopping with my mother in a big store. We went on the elevator.

T: Who worked the elevator?

C: An elevator man, and he told what the floors were, and what they sold there.

T: Would you like to run the elevator? You tell us where you're starting and we'll ride with you.

C: Start on the ground.

T: The ground floor—it's also called the first floor. Boys and girls, are you ready? Is some part of you ready to go up?

(Teacher helps the "elevator man" to start the scale song; the child may improvise words on each step. The rest of the class follows the movement.)

(Each child decides which way to go, where to begin, whether to stop at each floor, or go "express." The teacher helps with the singing of appropriate parts of the scale songs.)

T: Listen as Rita plays. ——— Which way are Jack and Jill going?

C: Up.

T: Now listen to my piece. (Chromatic scale, ascending.)
Did it go up or down?

C: Up.

T: Can you sing the Jack and Jill song as I play?

C: No.
It doesn't fit.
It went up.

T: There are different ways of going up?

C: Yes.

T: How about this way? (Plays major scale.) Sing the Jack and Jill song if it fits. ———

T: How about this one?

C: No.

T: And this?

C: Oh no!

T:

C: They're coming down.
T: Then sing with it. ——
   Listen to this one.

C: No.

Provide many opportunities for individual children to play scale songs on the melody bells or the piano. Middle C may be marked with colored plastic tape to permit more independent exploration. Sometimes you may help by asking, "Will you go up or down? Where will you begin?" Sing the words of a scale song, or "We're going up up up/ down down down. . . ."

Guide the child to discover that he can locate the start of the going-down song by noticing its relation to the group of two black keys on the piano. Later, the middle C need not be marked.

The Little Man Who Wasn't There[8]

T: Listen to this song:

As I was go-ing up the stair I met a man who was-n't there!

He was-n't there a-gain to-day! I wish, I wish he'd stay a-way.

[8] This poem was originally set to the natural minor scale by William S. Haynie. It appears in Eunice Boardman and Beth Landis: *Exploring Music: Kindergarten.* New York: Holt, Rinehart and Winston, 1969. Used by permission.

T: Can you show how the song goes as I sing? ———

C: It goes up.
Up the stairs.

T: Who was going up the stairs?

C: A man.
No.

T: Would you like to hear it again? ——— Who was going up?

C: You.
The man wasn't there.
It's silly.
The man was a "pretend."

T: You are right; it's a funny kind of "pretend" song. But one thing is certain; it goes—

C: Up.

T: Let's sing each step together with a long "la" and listen carefully. (Sing the natural minor scale in whole notes.) Can you come down? ———

C: It's a different way—not Jack and Jill.

T: Right, it's a different way.

C: It's the funny man way.
It's the *no* man way.

T: Perhaps you can find it on the piano later. Let's sing it once more. (Lead the song somewhat slower as children indicate its direction with their arms.)

C: It sounds scary.
Maybe it's a ghost.
Ghosts can't hurt you.
They're just pretend.

> Mark the A below middle C as a starting place on the piano. (See suggestions under *Ladder Melodies*.) "Always sing the song as you play; then you can find the piano sounds to match." The whole note version is preferable. It can be played with alternate index fingers, one (and only one) key is down at a time. "Play gently and smoothly and hear how the piano helps you sing."

On a Level

T: Now the melody bells will tell you how to move. Close your eyes and listen.

Which way did the music go?

C: Up.

T: Then where must you start?

C: (Demonstrating) Low.

T: I'll play the same thing again. Sing along softly as you move with the bells. ———— Now try these: listen the first time, get ready, and move with the music the second time I play.

———— ———— ———— (General confusion.)

Listen again. ———— Did the sounds go down?

C: No.

T: Did the sounds go up?

C: No.

T: What happened?

C: They stayed still.

They stayed in the same place.

T: Yes, we can say they stayed *on a level*.

Are these on a level?

C: Yes.

T: And these?

C: They went down.

T:

C: They went down.

T: Really? Listen:

C: *They* went down.
T: And what about these:

C: On a level.

T: Each one has a chance to play; you can make your music go up or down or stay on a level. Everyone turns away from the bells to listen.
C:

C: (Others.) It jumped all around!
T: It certainly did.
C:

C: (Others.) On a level.
T: Were they right?
C: Yes!

Ritsch Ratsch

C: You said we could sing *Ritsch Ratsch* for everybody—the song we sang in the play yard.
You help us.
T: I'll be glad to; that's one of my favorite songs.

Ritsch ratsch fi - li bom bom bom, fi - li bom bom bom, fi - li bom bom bom

Ritsch ratsch fi - li bom bom bom, fi - li bom bom bom, fi - li bom.

What did we hear this morning that made me think of the song?

C: Mr. J's rake made the scratchy sound against the sidewalk. We sang it for his work.

And when I was pushing Marisol in the swing you sang it. And when the swing was twisting with nobody in it. (Child demonstrates.)

T: Dorothy is twisting as if she were the swing. You try it.

How many twisting swings can we have?

Dorothy, please do it again. ——— Notice that she doesn't move her feet.

C: And her arms are up; they are the ropes of the swing.

T: Everybody twist and sing. ———

C: Your arms can twist, too.

T: Yes, they can. What else can we do with *Ritsch Ratsch?*

C: Push the swing.

Pull the rake.

First you push, then you pull.

T: Good, Shelley; push and pull—anything you like. And sing. ———

Notice how Abraham makes his whole body help his hands and arms.

C: And he changes his feet.

T: Yes; he pushes so far and so hard, he stands on one foot and then on the other. He must be pushing a very heavy bunch of—

C: Nothing! (General merriment.)

T: Everyone do it. (Leads the song slower and louder than before.) What happens to our song when we work very hard like that?

C: It's slow and heavy.

It's loud.

T: It is slow and loud. What will you do when I sing the song this way? (Sings very fast, softly. Children respond appropriately.) And this way? (Slowly and very softly.)

Hiney Matov (Complete)

T: Here is another part of the Hebrew song, a second melody; everybody sings it together. (Sings, designing the melody in the air.)

Hin-ey ma tov u-ma na-im, She-vet a-chim gam ya-chad.

How did the melody go?

C: It went up and down.

T: Yes, smoothly up and down, except for one place that is different. Sing it with me; see if you can find that place. (Repeat, stopping after "naim.") What happened?

C: It went up.
It went up all of a sudden.

T: Yes. Let's sing that little part. ("Naim.") How can you show that? Find a way to show that special place. (Several children crouch low and jump up at "naim.") You knew exactly where to come up. Let's sing the whole melody. Can you show how the other parts go smoothly? Show the going-up and down with any part of you—and sing. ———
Sally and Rosalind are singing and moving together, holding hands; that's very nice. Choose a friend and let's sing it one more time.

T: This is the third melody of *Hiney Matov,* the third part of the song. It uses the same words again. (Teacher sings, clapping the beat, starting very slowly and deliberately, and increasing the speed to very fast. The children join in the clapping, which breaks off with the singing.)

You followed very well! What happened to the music?

C: It got faster and faster.

T: How did it start?

C: With big slow claps.

T: Show us, Abraham.
Let's all do it that way, it's so much fun! ———

T: Now we're ready to put the three melodies together, one after the other. After that, we sing the echo part again, but not the same way.

EXAMPLES OF MUSIC EXPERIENCES   99

You'll know just how to sing if you listen to my part very carefully. First the echoing, then the smooth part we sing together and show with our hands in the air, and then the clapping part, and then we echo again. (On returning to the echos, start very softly, increasing to very loud for "gam ya-chad.") What happened?

C: It got louder and louder.

T: How would it sound if we started loud—

C: And got softer and softer.

T: Shall we try? ———

C: It sounds like everybody is going away.

T: Which way do you like it best? (Assorted comments.) How will you know which way to sing?

C: Listen.

Pay attention.

Listen and be ready to echo.

John, the Rabbit

Oh John, the rab-bit, Yes, ma'am. Had a might-y hab-it, Yes, ma'am.

Jump-in' in my gar-den, Yes, ma'am. Cut-tin' down my cab-bage, Yes, ma'am.

My sweet po-ta-toes, Yes, ma'am. My ripe to-ma-toes, Yes, ma'am,

And if I live,— Yes, ma'am. To see next fall,— Yes, ma'am.

I ain't gon-na have,— Yes, ma'am. No cot-ton at all, Yes, ma'am.

(General discussion: farm, farmer, vegetable garden, cabbage, sweet potatoes, tomatoes; rabbit, where he lives—not in a cage or pen, what he eats, how he gets it. Contrast with how *person* lives, eats, and so on.)

T: Have you ever seen a real rabbit?
C: In the pet store window.
T: How did he hop? ——— That's fine, Amy, with both feet. Good Joannie. Watch Amy and Joannie.

Hop, hop, hop, hop, hop, hop, hop, hop.

Everybody hop with Amy and Joannie. (Teacher hops, too.)

Hop, hop, hop, hop, hop, hop, hop, hop.

T: If the Mother Rabbit was not in a pen, if she had lots of room in the field or in the woods, how do you think she would hop? (Children experiment with larger hops, at X's in next example, some crouching low.)

Yes, ma'am yes, ma'am yes, ma'am yes, ma'am.

We have so many Mother and Father Rabbits, I would feel sorry for the farmer if you all got into his garden! If I play ♩ ♩ on the drum, how will you hop? ——— Yes, little hops. And if I play ♩ 𝄾 ♩ 𝄾 ? ——— Fine. Suppose I stop; what will you do?

C: Stop.
 And listen!
T: Do you think rabbits are good listeners? Why?
C: They have big ears.
T: They certainly do; but is that enough? Can they just sit and wait?
C: They have to pay attention.
 They must be ready to hop.
T: Then you do, too, for whatever you hear. (Play the Quick Response Game, with ♩, ♩ 𝄾 , and stops.)

T: Help me sing the song as you rest from hopping; remember to be ready with the "Yes ma'am's." ———
 I guess Henry, the Rabbit wasn't tired. Did you notice? He hopped the "Yes ma'am's" every time just when you sang them! Let's all try that.

———— (Some children need to sing or say the "Yes, ma'am's" with the hops.) How else could a rabbit show the "Yes ma'am's?"

C: A rabbit doesn't make any sound, but he could move his mouth.

T: Show us how.

C: It's his nose that moves.

T: How? (Children experiment.) Can you do that just at the "Yes ma'am" places? ————

Fine! What else can you do for the "yes ma'am's?" It could be something that a rabbit *can't* do.

C: Clap hands.

Play on the drum.

(Individual children respond in various ways with ♫ ≀ or ♩ ≀ for each "Yes ma'am.")

In order to hop accurately, that is, land exactly on the beat, one must actually start the movement before the beat. The children can pick this up from your demonstration: exaggerate the down-up knee action on the last eighth note of the measure,

The child who can respond accurately in body movement without singing the "yes ma'am's" out loud is relying on his *inner hearing* (a term used by Dalcroze)—his aural image of the previously sung phrases. As he supplies the unsung beat in movement, his attention is focused on the on-going quality of the music.

Jim-a-long Josie I

Hey, jim-a - long,_ jim-a-long Jo-sie, Hey, jim-a - long,_ jim-a-long Joe.

(For "Hey," substitute "Walk," "Jump," "Run.")

T: You've "jim-a-longed" many different ways with your feet, can you "jim-a-long" with your hands? What can they do?

C: They can clap.

T: Let's. (Sing the song with "Clap.")

What makes the sound?

C: One hand hits the other hand.

T: Show us how you clap, Edmund.

C: (Claps hard.) It hurts your hands.

T: You need not hit so hard. Try it more gently, and separate your hands quickly—just as soon as they meet. You may like the sound better, too. (Children experiment.) See Shirley clap; her hands bounce away from each other. That's the idea. Try it that way, everyone; let's sing the song with this easy, bouncy clap. ———
Charlie has a different clap; show us, Charlie. He's making a circle with

each hand, and the two circles meet for the clap. (Claps $\downarrow$'s, right hand clockwise, left hand counter clockwise.)

The big circles help you fit right in with the song. Can you make the circles go the other way? Everybody try clapping that way as we sing. ———

Tommy has still another clap. Listen to the sound he makes.
(Arms going straight up and down, in opposite directions.)

C: It makes a swishy sound.
It's like playing the cymbals.

T: Little ones, or great big ones?

C: Great big ones.

T: Everybody try it. That's right; your arms go very far apart.

Let's sing ——— (clap is $\downarrow$).
Now, can you clap like the tiny cymbals? (clap is $\downarrow$).
Close your eyes and listen to Shelley. When you know what size cymbals she is "playing," you can join her. ——— (Take turns doing this.)

T: Shirley is "playing" a very big pair of cymbals. (No singing.) Can you "play" along with her on the small ones? How many of your sounds to each one of Shirley's? ——— Now, let's try it the other way. Andy, you start us off with the small ones. ———

T: You've been clapping in front of you. Now, can you clap in a different place? (Experiment. Stretching, bending, and twisting of the torso permit clapping "everywhere" in space—high above the head, close to the floor, around one leg or the other, reaching toward a wall.)

T: Choose a different place to clap as we sing. You may want to change to still another place while you're singing. The song may tell you when. ———

C: You change when it says "clap."

T: That sounds like a good idea, Jimmy; we'll try it. ———

Wake Me!

Wake me! Shake me! Don't let me sleep too late. Got - ta get up bright an' ear - ly in the morn - in', Swing on the gar - den gate.

T: Who wakes you in the morning?
C: I wake myself.
    I hear my mother in the kitchen.
    My mother calls me.
T: Why does the person in the song want to be up "bright and early?"
    Listen. (Repeat song.)
C: To swing on the garden gate.
T: Is that what *you* like to do early in the morning?
C: I don't have a gate.
    You have to have a yard to have a gate.
    I like to eat breakfast with my daddy.
    I like to play with my dog.
    I like to see if it is snowing.
T: Even if you don't have a garden gate, you don't want to be a lazy-bones, do you? Can we sing the song together? (Some children do not sing with the teacher; instead they echo during the rests after "Wake me" and "Shake me.") I heard some nice echoes. But the song won't let you echo all the way through. You'll have to listen carefully to find out where you can. (Repeat, a bit slower, helping children to echo two words on the rests, clapping twice at the end of the song.) I wonder if you could clap all the way through, so gently there's no sound—but louder in all the echo places; then you could sing all of the words with me. ———— How many out-loud claps each time?
C: Two.
T: Good! Sing with me and we'll clap two claps in each of the right places. ———— Sandy has a different way to do it. Show us, Sandy. (He slaps each knee.)

C: Each hand has a knee.
   Two knees, two claps.

T: Everybody try it. If you sing you'll find the right times easily. ——
   What could you do instead of clapping or slapping? What other sounds
   could you make, your own self? (Cluck tongue, pat floor with foot, . . .)
   What motion can you make, just in the right places? (Wave hand,
   twist hips, bend and straighten knees.)

T: Can you make an instrument play the two sounds for you? (Children
   experiment with nonpitched percussion instruments.) Can you find the
   bell [or key on the piano] that sounds like the beginning of the song?
   (Children match the tone.) How will it sound if you play all the echoes
   there? —— Did you like it?

C: Yes.
   It stays on a level.

T: The whole song?

C: Just the echoes.

Jingle Bells

T: Several people have asked to play the listening game. Who remembers
   what to do?

C: You close your eyes.
   You must be very still.

T: And save your answers until the talking time. Ready? (Teacher se-
   cretly places a bracelet of jingle bells in her smock pocket. She moves
   so that they sound.) What did you hear?

C: Jingling.
   Jingle bells.

T: Really? I wonder where they are. (Moves again.)

C: In your pocket.
   You hid them in your pocket.

T: Well, so they are! Would you like to try them? (They experiment,
   shaking the bells.) What really makes the bells sound?

C: They have little things inside.
   Little metal things.
   You have to shake the bells.

T: What does that do to the little metal things inside?

C: They hit the bells.

T: Watch and listen. (Teacher moves the bells very slowly and carefully
   through the air.) Did you hear anything? Why didn't they sound?

C: The little things are not hitting.

You have to go faster.

T: You certainly have to make the bells move back and forth, or up and down, or in some shape to make the little metal things inside hit the bells—that is, if you want them to sound. I wonder if you can move yours so carefully that they do not sound! Anyone can make the bells sound—that's very easy. But you must be very clever to move them *quietly!* (Gives each child a ring of bells.) Move everywhere in the room, but ever so gently. Now find a place and sit down, and put your bells on the floor in front of you. You were so careful, I heard only a few faint jingles. ——— Look at the bells; what is the shape of the band?

C: It's round.
   It's a circle.

T: What song do you know about a round thing.

C: "There's a little wheel a-turning."

T: How can you make the wheels go around? (Experiment.) Try to do it without lifting the bells from the floor.
   Several people found a good way: put one finger on the floor in the center of the ring, and draw wheels with that finger. Let's sing the song and make the bells jingle that way. ——— Now I'm sure you know another song—about bells!

Jin-gle bells, jin-gle bells, jin-gle all the way,

Oh what fun it is to ride in a one-horse o-pen sleigh,—

Jin-gle bells, jin-gle bells, jin-gle all the way,

Oh what fun it is to ride in a one horse o-pen sleigh.—

T: The song says it's fun to ride "in a one-horse open sleigh." Have you ever been for a ride in one? What *is* a "one-horse open sleigh?"

C: You slide on the snow in a sled, down the hill, in the park. And you have to walk up.

That's a sled. Santa Claus has a sleigh; it's bigger and horses pull it.

He doesn't have horses, he has reindeer.

He could have horses if he wanted them.

T: Who pulls the sleigh in the song?

C: One horse.

T: Yes; I brought a picture to show you.

C: Lots of people are in the sleigh.

T: How can the horse pull so many?

C: The snow is slippery.

A horse is very strong.

T: Those are good reasons. Look at the picture; where do you see the jingle bells?

C: On the horse's head.

They're tied to his bridle.

T: This part (indicating) is called the bridle. The part on his head is called the crownpiece. Can you keep your jingle bells on your head—with nothing to tie them to? ———— How can we make them stay? Look at Charlie. He has one finger on his head, in the circle, just as we did on the floor. Trot, Charlie, and let's see if the bells stay on your head. ———— They do! Let's all try it. (Sing and trot.)

T: Suppose you are in the house, in the country, and the horse is still in the barn; would you hear the bells?

C: No.

T: Would you hear the driver if he were singing?

C: Maybe, if he sings very loud. (Demonstrates by screaming; some children cover ears.)

T: Is that singing?

C: He's screaming; it hurts my ears.

T: Maybe the driver of the sleigh will start to sing as he leaves the barn to come to the house. Let's try to make the sound of the song and the bells coming toward us. How shall we begin—softly or loud?

C: So you can't hear.

T: Ever so gently! (Sing the song and shake the bells in a gradual crescendo, flinging the hand upward for the last octave skip.) What fun! I could hear him coming closer and closer, couldn't you? Now suppose we're standing right by the horse; the driver starts the horse and sleigh back to the barn. Let's hear what happens. (Sing with gradual decrescendo.) (Several children accent the top of the octave skip.) What happened?

C: It got softer and softer, and then there was a surprise!

T: Sandy is wearing the bells on his arm. Where else could you wear them? (Children experiment, putting bells on ankles, around big toes, hanging from hooked thumbs. They trot and sing, deciding each time whether to get softer or louder.)
What happened that time?

C: The music got louder, little by little.

T: And at the end. (Sings octave skip on "sleigh.")

C: It went up.

T: Let's sing it again; what other words could you use?

C:

Low   high

The Rock Island Line

T: (After a game of Follow the Leader.) If everyone has had a chance, I think it is my turn now. Are you ready? (Teacher claps very slowly, using large circular arm movements; accelerates, retards, adjusting the size of the movements.)[9]

C: It gets faster and faster. A train gets faster and faster.

T: Can you be a train, and do that with your feet? The piano will be the engineer; it will tell you when to start and how to speed up, and when to stop. (Alternate hands play tone clusters, such as:)

C: The train has a lot of cars.
They're hitched together.

T: If each of you is a car, you can make a train. How will you hitch the cars? (Children hold at shoulders or waist.) You can be an engine with

[9] The children have seen and heard Golden MacDonald and Leonard Weisgard, *Whistle for the Train,* New York: Doubleday, 1956 and Lois Lenski, *The Little Train,* New York: Henry Z. Walck, 1940.

no cars attached to it, if you would rather. Ready? We'd better think ahead; suppose we come to a semaphore that is like this. (Arms out straight.) What must the train do?

C: Stop.

T: And when the "arms" are up straight?

C: Go.

C: I want to be the semaphore.

T: Then stand where I can see you, Rita, and the piano will follow your commands. You who are the train need not watch Rita—just listen to the piano to know what to do. Are you a passenger train or a freight train? (Discussion.) ———

Oh, the Rock Is - land Line__ is a might - y good road,__

Oh, the Rock Is - land Line__ is the road to ride,__

Oh, the Rock Is - land Line__ is a might - y good road,__

If you want to ride you got - ta take it like you find it

Fine

Buy your tick - et at the sta - tion for the Rock Is - land Line.__

Now I may be right and I may be wrong,__

D.C. al Fine

But you're gon - na miss me when I'm gone.__

(Improvised "chug's" and Part A are used for movement; stop to listen
through Part B, move again during repeated A part.)

T: Which part of the song is this? (Plays B part.)
C: The part where we stop and wait.
   The semaphore is down.
T: And when you hear the "chug's?"
C: The train goes again.

Jim-a-long Josie II

T: What is this part of the song saying? What is the last word?

Hey, jim - a - long,___ jim - a - long, Jo - sie.

C: "Josie."
T: And this one? (Sings second phrase with "la's.")
C: "Joe."
T: (Continues with phrases three and four.) Sometimes it's "Josie" and
   sometimes it's "Joe."
C: It takes turns.
T: Can you say a lot of "Josie's" with your feet? ———— Now some
   "Joe's." ———— What are these? (Teacher plays on woodblock.)
C: "Joe's."
T: And these? ————
C: "Josie's."
T: The woodblock will play "Joe's" or "Josie's." Let your feet tell which
   is which. (Quick Response Game, with stops.)
   Now listen to this:

C: (Galloping.) I'm a horse.
   I'm a pony.
   I can skip. (Some skip.)
T: What does "hey" mean?
C: Like in "Hey jim-a-long?"
T: Yes, or if I say "Hey, Rosalind."
C: Hi.
   Hello.
T: Then wave to your friend as we sing *Hey Jim-a-long*. ———— Johnny is

"waving" with his feet; we had better move! "Walk jim-a-long. . . . (All walk and sing.) Listen; how many times does the song say "walk?" (Teacher sings song.)

C: Four.

T: Each time you sing "walk," turn to a different place in the room. Ready? ———
   Can you find another way to move? Yes; let's jump with Lynn. ———
   Julia is jumping on one foot.

C: I am hopping.

T: Good. Everyone hop and sing. Notice how Steve keeps his other foot high off the floor. And Sandy is holding his other foot so it can't go down. Perhaps you would like to try that. (Teacher adjusts the tempo to the speed of the hops.) (Some children sit down.) Now Johnny is really waving with his feet—so fast. Can you? ——— If you stand up and do that, what happens?

C: You run. (All sing "Run jim-a-long . . ." with tempo adjusted to movement.)

Looby Loo

T: John, you look just like Cowboy Small.[10] Listen to the sound of his feet, everyone. Gallop some more, John. ——— How did his feet sound?

C:

T: Can you make the same sound with your hands? Everyone sit down and try it. ——— (Children are sitting down.) Watch Elliott; he's clapping on one thigh, then on the other. Let's close our eyes and listen. Do it again, Elliott.

C: It sounds like galloping.

T: Why? How does galloping sound?

C: One hand is harder than the other.

T: One hand hits harder than the other? Let me try.

C: That's not galloping.

T: I made one harder.

[10] Lois Lenski, *Cowboy Small—Vaquero Pequeno*, New York: Henry Z. Walck, 1960.

C: It doesn't sound like the horse galloping.

T: I'll do it slower. You listen carefully; maybe we can find out what's wrong. ———

C: That hand (pointing to the unaccenting one) has to be faster.

T: I'll try. ———

C: Yes.

The hard one is longer.

T: That's right. Everybody try it.

♪ ♩ ♪ ♩

Short long short long . . . . . (Children join in.)

Spirited songs in six-eight time usually lend themselves to galloping or skipping. The rhythm of the skip is represented ♩ ♪, *long-short* in a two to one relationship. (An occasional group of three eighths adds to the élan.) A series of ♩. ♪ 's, *long-short's* in a three to one relationship, can also be appropriate for skipping or galloping, depending on the tempo of the song. Emphasizing the shortness of the sixteenth note makes this a livelier rhythm.

T: Does a horse always gallop?
C: Sometimes he trots.
T: Show us how. ——— Make that sound with your hands, can you?
——————
C: It's running.
   They're all short.

T: Here's a song for horses and ponies, and for skipping girls.

Here we go loo - by loo, here we go loo - by lye

Here we go loo - by loo, all on a Sat - ur - day night.____ *Fine*

I put one hand in, I put one hand out

I give my - self a shake, shake, shake, and turn my - self a - bout. *D. C. al Fine*

(Returns to A Part.) So we have a galloping part.

C: And then the part where you "put" something. And then it gallops again.

T: If the horse were in the stable, and you were in the house, how would the song start? Let's make the horse get closer and closer. (Children experiment with various dynamic plans.)

T: What would you do if the middle part sounded like this?

la   la . . . .

(Children trot.) Can we find some trotting words?
(Discussion, including rhyming possibilities.)

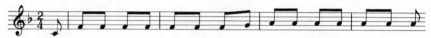

Oh, pon - ies like to   trot trot trot, The pon - ies like to   trot trot trot,

They trot trot trot   and trot trot trot, They like to   trot a   lot lot lot.

Another ending: They stop right on the dot.

(Quick Response Game: The teacher sings different endings; children stop on "dot.")

This time, then, we'll have a galloping part, then—

C: A trotting part.

And then the galloping part again. ————

T: We had another song that was the same in the beginning and end, and different in the middle. Who knows it? Do you need a hint? We stood still and listened in the different part.

C: The train song!

There's a Little Wheel

There's a lit-tle wheel__ a-turn-in' in my heart

There's a lit-tle wheel__ a-turn-in' in my heart

In my heart_____ in my heart_____

There's a lit-tle wheel__ a-turn-in' in my heart.

T: The song says there's a wheel turning; how does a wheel turn?

C: (Demonstrating.) Round and round.

In a circle. (They describe circles of various sizes—with the arm, fore-arm, and with a finger, as the teacher sings the song again.)

T: Look at Amy's wheel. Can you make a wheel the same way, with your whole arm? And let's all sing. (Adjusts tempo to movement.) Where did we see some wheels about that size yesterday?

C: On the bus that took us to the zoo.

T: Yes! And do you remember seeing an even bigger wheel?

C: Where the men were working on the building, and the pipe was on the spool that was taller than the men.

T: That was telephone cable on that tremendous spool. Can you make a circle that big—a great big wheel? Let's try. Reach as high as you can, on your tip-toes, then way over to the side; sweep your arm down to the floor, and then way over to the other side. Good! Let's sing. (Ad-justs tempo.) "There's a great big wheel. . . ."

That was fine. Now, I wonder who can find a real wheel right in this room. (Children find wheels on toy tractors and trucks.) Can you show a very small wheel like that? (Experiment, tracing around the toy wheels with fingers.) What a tiny wheel Joannie found! Let's make tiny wheels in the air as we sing. "There's a little tiny wheel. . . ."

T: I saw your wheels turning nicely with the song. See what Andy's wheel is doing! Watch Andy; his wheel goes first one way, then the other. Let's all try it as we sing. (Some children naturally change direction at each phrase-end.) Let's watch Andy and John and change when they do. ———— Did you like doing it that way? How did you know when to change?

C: When the song said the same thing again, I changed.
    When you say "heart," you change.

T: Everyone's wheel was turning in front of him; where else could yours turn?

C: Behind you.
    On the side of you.

T: This time, when we sing, try to find places where you've never turned a wheel before. You may want to change places, as John did, every time you sing "heart." (Elicit crossing over to turn a wheel on the other side, turning the wheel with your other hand, changing hands to show the phrasing, having both hands draw wheels at the same time.)

T: What do you call the shape of a wheel?

C: Round.
    A circle.

T: Can you make a circle? ———— If each person holds hands with two different friends, what will happen? Keep doing that, until there are no empty hands. ———— What shape did we make?

C: A big circle!

T: Drop your hands. ———— Now everybody can help the circle go around as we sing.

C: The big circle should go the other way at "heart."

T: Good idea! Each person must listen as we sing, and help the circle change. (After discussing the way the clock's hands move, the children use the term "clockwise," imaging the clock face on the floor; later they learn "counter-clockwise.") (Later, the children explore and discover squares and triangles, forming them with their bodies. Individual children are straight lines; others help shift them into position. Individual children also suggest shapes of letters that one person alone can make— I, V, T, Y.)

T: How high can you make your wheels? Shelley is drawing wheels on the ceiling—almost! Let's all do that. Stretch your legs; you'll have to be up on your tip-toes. Stretch your whole body as tall as it will stretch, and your arms, too.

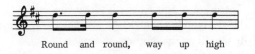

Round and round, way up high

Now, how low can you make your wheels? ——— Chippy's are flat
on the floor. Let's sing down low.

Round and round, way down low

(Individual children direct the group, by action or by singing directions.)

T: "Oh I feel so very happy in my heart. . . ." (All sing.)
    Do you feel happy? You *look* happy. How can I tell?
C: We're smiling.
T: Yes, and there's a bounce in your step. Can you also look angry? How
    does an angry person look? ——— I wonder if you could sing the
    happy song and look angry at the same time? ——— Does the song
    still sound happy? How did you change it?
C: It's slower.
    It's louder.
    You kind of shout it.
    The words are wrong.
T: No one seems to be able to look very angry and sound very happy at
    the same time. Just for now, let's pretend we are very angry. Think how
    it must really feel to be very angry. Do you remember someone who
    was very angry?
C: The peddler who wanted to sell the caps, and the monkeys took
    them.[11]
T: Yes! What did the peddler say?
C: "You monkeys, you—you give me back my caps!"
T: My, you do sound angry; can you make the drum "say" that?
C:

T: What makes Richard sound so angry on the drum?

[11] Esphyr Slobodkina, *Caps For Sale,* New York: William R. Scott, 1960.

C: The drum is growly, and it's loud and jerky.

T: How would it sound on the wood block? You may try, Elliott. ——

C: It sounds angry, but not growly.

It sounds mean.

T: Daisy wants to try it on the triangle. What do you think? ——

C: It doesn't sound angry at all! You can't make it jerky.

It's not growly or mean.

It sounds very nice.

(A general discussion and exploration follows, of how to make "happy" sounds on the instruments. The children decide to sing "Oh I feel so very happy." On the first try, everyone plays, drums and triangles, with each beat of the music.)

T: I can't hear the words; can you?

C: Hardly.

T: What can you do? Don't you think we should hear the words? (Children sing louder and bang on the instruments.) Do you like that sound?

C: We should play softer.

T: That deserves a try, Kenny. Try to play ever so gently when you sing the words; listen for them. Perhaps the triangles could just *pretend* to play during the singing, and save all of their playing for where the words *aren't*. (The triangles' "orchestration" serves as punctuation between the phrases. Later, the drums play only on the important beats.)

Rig-a-jig-jig

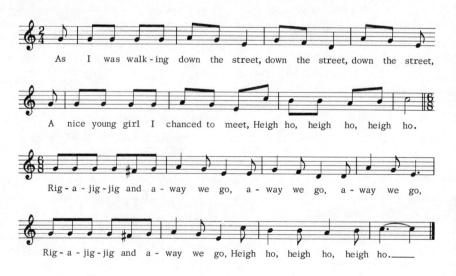

As I was walk-ing down the street, down the street, down the street,

A nice young girl I chanced to meet, Heigh ho, heigh ho, heigh ho.

Rig - a - jig - jig and a - way we go, a - way we go, a - way we go,

Rig - a - jig - jig and a - way we go, Heigh ho, heigh ho, heigh ho.___

C: The words tell you what to do.
   You walk.
T: And when the song says "Rig-a-jig-jig?" Find what fits. ⸺
C: You can gallop.
   Skip.
T: Either one. Shall we try the whole song? ⸺ You can do something else with the "Rig-a-jig-jig" part; you can jig! Do you know how to jig? (Demonstrates.) Lots of people used to dance the jig. I believe they still do in the country called Ireland. Then it is called the Irish jig. It's easy to do: just jump, then hop. ⸺ Now you can make your own jig steps. Put your jumping feet in different places, and when you hop (on one foot) the other foot can go up in front or up in back. ⸺. See how Dorothy's hops are first on one foot, then on the other.

Rig — a — jig —	jig and a — way	we go
Jump	Left	Jump	Right
	foot		foot
	hop		hop

Everybody try it. ⸺ Let's do the whole song. In the walking part, go anywhere in the room. Wave to your friend when you pass him by. Then do your jig wherever you happen to be.
C: And then walk again. ⸺

T: What will you do if you hear:

la   la · · · ·

And this?

la   la   la · · · ·

What about this:

la   la · · · ·

And this?

la   la · · · ·

(Most walk, a few run.) Some people are running. Does it fit?

C: Yes.

T: Does running fit the whole first part? Let's try. ——— So you can run *or* walk.

C: I like to run.
   It says "walk."

T: Those who want to walk stay in the center of our space. The runners get close to the edges. Runners, please go clockwise.

C: And we'll walk counterclockwise!

T: Try it. And what will happen at the "Rig-a-jig-jig?"

C: Everybody do a jig.

Ev'rybody Loves Saturday Night

C: Tomorrow there's no school.

T: Why?

C: Because it's Saturday.
   Every Saturday I go to the supermarket with my mother.
   Sunday I'm going to my grandmother's.
   Saturday and Sunday are not school days.

T: What are the school days? ——— And then there's the week-end, Saturday and Sunday, when you do different things. That reminds me of a song.

Mo - fe mo - ni s'mo ho___ gbe - ke.___

Mo - fe mo - ni, mo - fe mo - ni, mo - fe mo - ni, mo - fe mo - ni,

Mo - fe mo - ni s'mo ho___ gbe - ke.___

C: What does it say?
   Is it Hebrew?

T: No, it's not Hebrew; it's the language of another far off country, a country called Sierra Leone. The country is in Africa. We can find it on our world globe.

C: My uncle was in Africa.

T: Maybe he knows the song, too. Listen to it again. ――――

C: What does it say?

T: You can sing this song with English words, too.

I have a friend who has been to Sierre Leone. He says that everybody loves Saturday night there because that is when they dance the High Life. High Life is the name of a dance.

C: Do the dance.

   How do you do your feet?

T: I don't know the step, but I do know that many African dancers like to move their shoulders and their hips. Why don't you try some ways to dance with your shoulders. We'll try the hips another time. ――――

   Fine. Notice Shelley has her shoulders going up and down together; Abraham has first one shoulder, then the other.

C: Like a see-saw.

T: Yes, and Dorothy made the see-saw movement twice as fast. Can you make one shoulder come out in front of you? ―――― Now the other.

   ―――― Very good. Let's sing the song; move your shoulders anyway you like. (Teacher claps on rests, starting with arms high, lower for each clap.)

C: I like the clapping.

T: Perhaps everyone would like to clap on that part.

   Let's try it together.

C: Your hands come down.

T: Why do my hands come down?

C: The "ev'rybody's" come down.

T: Is John right? Listen carefully, and try it for yourself. ———— (General agreement.) How would you clap if I sang,

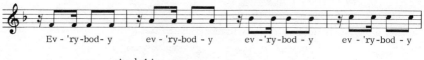

Ev - 'ry-bod- y   ev - 'ry-bod - y   ev -'ry-bod - y   ev - 'ry-bod - y

———— And this way,

Ev-'ry-bod-y ev-'ry-bod-y   Ev-'ry-bod-y ev-'ry-bod-y ev-'ry-bod-y

———— And this way? (As in song.) ————

C: That's the right way.
T: That's how it is in this song. Are you ready to sing and do your shoulder dance? We'll all clap together when the song tells us to. ————
C: It's another "different in the middle" song.
T: You're right, Andy! But I wonder: are the beginning and the end *exactly* the same? Listen; here's the beginning. Follow with your hand. (Sings with "la.") And here's the end; follow with your hand. ————
C: It's different.
    It leans down and comes back.
T: That's a very good way to describe it, Andy. It goes down a very small step and comes back. That's not what happens in the first part, is it? You heard the difference, but I think we could still call it a "different in the middle" song, as Andy suggested, because the beginning of each part is the same, and the words are the same.
C: And we are shoulder dancing the same.
    We sang the first part twice; why don't we sing the coming back part twice?
T: Let's try it. ———— (Only a few repeat the last phrase.)
C: It sounds finished with one time.
    We made an echo.
T: I liked that! Didn't you? You were a good echo!

T: I have a question to ask you. What is the word in the song that sounds for a long time, longer than all of the others? Let's try to find it. (They begin to sing.)
C: "Night!"
T: Yes, "night"; how can you be sure to sing all of it?
C: You move your shoulders while you sing it.
T: How many times? You sing the song and we'll watch your shoulders.

C: Four.
   Two of each shoulder.
T: Right, either way. You can count it to yourself, or just enjoy the shoulder dance at that place so you won't rush away.

A child exploring at the piano (or melody bells) may easily find the outline of the melody.

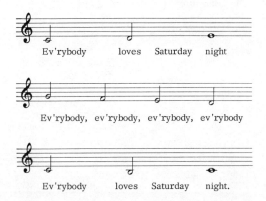

Ev'rybody   loves   Saturday   night

Ev'rybody, ev'rybody, ev'rybody, ev'rybody

Ev'rybody   loves   Saturday   night.

You may help by focusing on one section of the song—singing it with him and reviewing the design in the air. Reassure him that his voice will tell him which way to go.

Attention to the main outline of the melody is sufficient. It is desirable as well. Playing repeated tones on the piano is difficult for a young child; he must release the key in order to play it again. Attention to this technical difficulty distracts from the flow of the music. Singing the song, or sections of it, *in tempo,* is essential to the musical experience.

You may challenge an interested youngster to find the same song beginning on the first of the three black keys (F sharp). By trial and error he discovers that the white keys he will use are just above and just below the black group of three. He will discover, also, that the Jack and Jill song (major scale) on F sharp uses the same white keys. When encouraged, some children will "find" songs or fragments of songs beginning on other keys. Over a period of time, they remember the families of keys needed for particular songs. These are viable experiences for acquiring the concept of *tonality*. (For the minor tonality, see *Little Man*.)

Hot Cross Buns

T: This morning Amy made a very interesting discovery. Would you like to tell the others, Amy?

C: The same music has different words.

T: Show us, Amy.

C: (Playing and singing)

Gam   ya - chad.
Three blind mice.
Hot   cross buns.

T: Can you sing with Amy, and show how the melody goes? ———— Very good. It goes—

C: Down.

T: I think you all know *Hot Cross Buns*. Is that part at the beginning or at the end of the song? (General disagreement.) If you follow the whole song as you sing it through, you can find out for sure.

Hot cross buns, hot cross buns; One a pen-ny, two a pen-ny, Hot cross buns.

C: The beginning and the end.
And another time.
You go down three times.
There's one different part.
I can play it.

T: All right, Joannie, do. (Child plays eighth notes somewhat laboriously.) Boys and girls, let's sing that part again. ———— Everyone, put one hand out and pretend it is the piano. Now, with one finger of the other hand, "play" that part as you sing. (The teacher sings lightly and in tempo with the children.)

C: The finger hops fast.

T: Yes, it only has time to tap the "piano" very gently.

C: The finger is hopping fast.
It's running.

T: Joannie, try it that way at the piano. ———— Fine. Did we decide how many "Hot cross buns" parts there were, going down?

C: Three.
Two and the different part and then another one.
Let me play the "Hot cross buns" part.

T: You may, Amy, and Joannie, you be ready with the running part. Everybody will sing with you. (The children play in different registers.) John is stepping the first pattern, "Hot cross buns." Who can step "One a penny, two a penny"? Decide to step one part or the other and do it as the girls play. ————

C: It's a different-in-the-middle song.

T: Right you are!

The descending melodic pattern of "gam yachad" is the ending of many other songs. You may guide the children to discover which songs they know that end in this way. Have them recognize the same melodic shape in fragments of unfamiliar songs that you play or sing for them. If you omit the last tone, the children will sing it unaided; this is the *home tone* (tonic).

A variety of other music learnings can evolve from further experiences with this simple melody:

Contrasting instruments may play the A and B parts, or two children may decide to "orchestrate" the first rhythmic pattern. (See "Making-Up" in Chapter 4.) Experiment with combinations of registers on the piano. Someone may discover that the phrases can be delineated by playing on the fourth beats of measures one, two, and four.

Challenge the children to find a variety of dynamic plans, using contrasting levels (*fortissimo* and *pianissimo*) or changing levels ("as if the music were moving away or coming close").

Orchestrate with solo and group singing. The contrast between the single voice and many focuses on the element of *texture*.

The third phrase may be played as sustained tones on the piano or melody bells if repeating the key is too difficult.

"How would the piece sound if there were no longer or

shorter sounds?" you may ask. Establish an on-going beat by walking with the children and singing one tone per step. "Which way do you prefer?" This kind of activity helps the children to analyze and appreciate the musical values of the rhythmic patterns.

Singing Conversation

T:

Boys and girls, boys and girls, boys and girls, please sit down

on the floor. It's fun to sing in-stead of talk.

Shall we? What did you do when it snowed and snowed?

C:

I played in the snow.

T:

Did you play by your-self?

C:

John-ny played with me.

T:

He did?

C:

Yes, he brought his sled to the park.

C: (Talking.) I have a sled.
T:

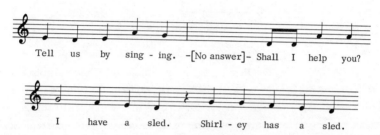

Tell us by sing - ing. -[No answer]- Shall I help you?

I have a sled. Shirl - ey has a sled.

C: (Another.)

I have a sled.

T:

Ev - 'ry - bod - y sing: I have a sled.

C:

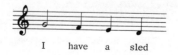

I have a sled

T:

What shall we do with our sleds?

C:

Climb up to the top of the hill.

T: Everybody sing.

Climb up to the top of the hill.

Practice singing imaginary conversations in private to overcome self-consciousness. In the beginning, you may find it helpful to say the words with exaggerated expression, noticing which ones are emphasized. Start singing the phrase on one pitch; show the important words by making them longer, later by making them higher. Conversely, you may choose to lower the pitch of unimportant words, or make them shorter.

Refer to other suggestions after *Echoing,* earlier in this chapter. Try scale lines, octave skips, and melodic fragments from songs; adjust them to the rhythm of your words.

Richard's Song

C: I made a song yesterday.

T: On our trip—I remember; on the bumpy bus. Please sing it for everybody.

C:

We're rid-ing on the bus, bump, bump, bump.

T: Sing it again, Richard—twice; and after I sing you a different part,
sing it once again. Ready?

C:

We're rid - ing on the bus, bump, bump, bump.

T:

Where are we go - ing?

C:

We're rid - ing on the bus, bump, bump, bump.

C: (Another)

We're go - ing to the zoo, bump, bump, bump.

T:

What will we see there?

C:

We're go - ing to the zoo, bump, bump, bump.

C:

Lions, ti - gers and mon - keys and birds

T:

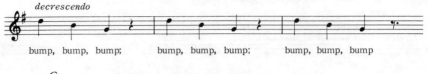

bump, bump, bump;   bump, bump, bump;   bump, bump, bump

C:

And   lots   of   oth - er   an - i - mals,   bump, bump, bump.

In subsequent sessions, much experimentation with instruments resulted in many different "orchestrations."

A part ("We're riding on the bus."): tambourine gently on the beats, *forte* on "bump bump bump."

Later, the drum was added on "bump bump bump."

B part ("Where are we going?"): shake the tambourine in a gradual crescendo.

Later, the triangle played ♩ 's, and subsequently

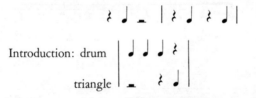

Repeated four times, with crescendo.

Used as an ending, with a decrescendo.

The instruments played, with no singing, at "bump bump bump."

VI

EVOLVING MUSIC TERMS AND NOTATION

The music experiences in Chapter 5 focused on *enactive* and *iconic* representations. Each child was involved with the elements of music as he moved his body, used his voice, and played simple instruments. He perceived sounds that were related to each other in different ways; after many experiences over a period of time he was able to organize his perceptions into concepts of the elements of music. He acquired skills that permitted him to use music as an expressive medium not only during music sessions but at other times during the day. In this way he formed concepts about his own experience of music as a source of spontaneity and self-satisfaction. While the main emphasis was on doing and imaging, *symbolic* representations were of course used.

Interaction in conversation as well as the words of songs are necessary for implementing music-movement experiences. Moreover, after vital encounters with music some children, usually at about the age of five, are curious about its notation. The timely introduction of terms and notation is an important aspect of planned musical growth. Understanding their place in the early stages of music learning can indicate some practical classroom strategies.

WORDS

Words used in music experiences fall into three general categories.

Lyrics

Foreign language lyrics and nonsense words are not in reality symbols of children's experiences. Even ordinary lyrics can be meaningless to children with limited (English) language experience in the beginning. However, all of these vocal sounds are excellent vehicles for developing skill in voice control, articulation, and aural discrimination. Repetition of the words usually defines the phrasing, thus facilitating the perception of design.

In action songs, the words direct the child as he sings and listens. This encouragement of simultaneous doing and hearing immediately involves him in a variety of musical experiences as it provides the vocabulary for transferring and extending his learning. It is this same strategy that the resourceful teacher develops through other songs. He helps the child to make connections between movement experiences and the words of the songs. He helps also to relate the expressive qualities of the music and the child's own feelings about the experiences. In effect he makes all songs into action songs.

Music has always been exploited as a means of memorizing words. It is far easier to remember what is sung than what is said. When classroom experiences make it possible for the child to analyze and correlate his actions, the sounds of the music and the sounds of the words, his language learning can be spectacular.

The teacher must know the lyrics well and enunciate them clearly as he sings, giving attention to appropriate tempo and dynamics. Children should not be pressured to sing; they learn the words gradually as they participate in movement. The teacher's demonstrated pleasure in singing and his enthusiastic participation in movement are contagious. They provide much of the children's motivation for learning the lyrics.

Classroom Conversation

Although the teacher moves and sings as a model in the classroom, some talking occurs as he elicits the children's physical responses. Conversely, while he encourages the children to move, play, and sing—to use music as an expressive medium—he is responsive to their comments about what they are doing and how they feel about their actions. He recognizes this verbal interaction as a way of helping them to organize their experiences and perceptions (aural and kinesthetic) into concepts *of* and *about* music. Their straightforward comments actually often afford him new insights into the nature of music.

In this conversation the child often finds a label for the concept he has formed.'When his physical behavior in games and quick response activities demonstrates that he has the concept, providing a name for it is helpful in evolving activities. It is crucial, however, that the emphasis remain on the musical experience. Some children are not ready to use the symbol; they need more experiences. Some who can supply the label one day may forget it before another day's session. The most effective approach, in any case, is to focus on *enactive* and *iconic* representations—the children's personal experience of the sound and movement that *are* the music—and provide the *symbolic* representation in the context of directions and comments.

Sometimes the teacher may use a term for a concept during an activity to focus attention on a child's performance or on this own demonstration because he finds it clumsy to circumvent the word itself. However, the child's understanding of the specific term is not crucial; he understands from the demonstrated action. For example, "Dorothy's arms make big circles, so they fit the slow beat of the music." "This gay song is livelier than the lullaby; the beat is faster." Some children derive the approximate meaning of *beat* from the context of the remarks. They explain their actions, "When you listen, you can keep clapping or walking to the music and it feels right." Later they recognize regular recurring accents, "When you're walking or clapping, some steps or claps want to be harder." They may show the resultant *meter* by swinging on the important beats.

When the sound stimulus is a recurring pattern of *long*'s and *short*'s, one child's accurate stepping of it can become the model for the group. "Short, short, l-o-n-g, short, short, l-o-n-g; that's it! You are stepping the *pattern*." Another child's enactment of the beat during this experience provides an opportunity for further clarification: "See, John is stepping the *beat*; it just keeps going. Amy is stepping the *pattern*—the *long*'s and *short*'s."

Although there can be no prescription for the exact moment to choose in supplying a musical term, the general tendency is for a verbally oriented adult to supply it too soon. Since such labels will have meaning only in terms of the children's experiences (see Chapter 5) the teacher may find it helpful to use a checklist of prerequisites: Have the children had many opportunities to represent the concept through body movement and the manipulation of instruments? Have they heard and sung a variety of songs and musical fragments that exemplify the concept? Have they had opportunities to translate given sounds into their own body movements? Have they experimented by providing appropriate sounds for movement patterns?

Delaying the use of terminology has an excellent side benefit. The teacher is forced to give musical directions for movement, and movement directions (gestures and demonstrated actions) for singing and playing. In this way he expands his music and movement repertoire and his use of these expressive nonverbal media.

MUSIC SYMBOLS

Music notation should be evolved as needed, with rich musical experiences always preceding its introduction. Starting with the simplest representations of separate musical elements, the rationale for writing it down should be clear—"so we can remember how the songs go," "so we can see what happens in the music," or "so we can sing your new song the same way tomorrow."

Often a child will draw a picture of a song, some representation of its subject. One such example can be the impetus for others, even for a picture collection of the class's repertoire, with song titles or beginning words added by the teacher or the children. A series of such pictures drawn on cardboards suggests a variety of listening games. For example, cards are distributed among the children; the teacher or a child sings a song, or a part of one, using "la's" instead of words; the child with the appropriate picture holds it high.

Lines and Pictures

When the focus has been on the songs' musical elements, it is not unusual for a child to show an obvious feature in some way. For example, *The Little Man* may be on steps. This can be the cue for the teacher's guidance.

T: Look at Shelley's[1] picture. What does it tell you about the *Little Man* song?

C: The music goes up the stairs.
But it needs more steps.

T: How many steps does it need? Suppose I sing it for you, and you count the steps. Ready? ———

C: It needs eight steps.

T: Shelley, will you show the steps on the chalkboard as we sing?

C:

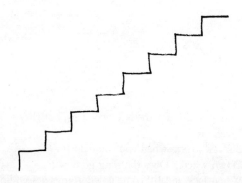

T: That's a good picture of the song. There's another way to show it. I think you will find it easier because you can write exactly what you sing right while you are singing it. Sing the song with me and I'll show you.

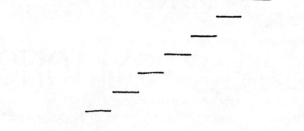

C: That's easy.
It's Jack and Jill going up the hill, too.

T: Is it? Let's try it and find out. We'll sing the song, Jennifer; you follow the going-up picture. ———

[1] Children in these samples have had a year of music-movement experiences.

C: It fits,
    No, it doesn't. There are two on each step.
T: How, Dorothy? Make another picture to show what you mean.
    We'll sing with you.
C:

    Only one line for the last two steps, but they're longer.
T: Excellent.
C: But it's wrong when you come down.
T: Down where? Does the song go down?
C: When Jack and Jill come down. (Sings descending scale, pointing right
    to left.)
T: Can you write your name, Dorothy?
C:

T: Are you sure you don't write it
C: That's backwards.

    You have to write from left to right.
T: And the same goes for music. So, can we go down this way? (Indicates
    right to left.)
C: No.
T: If the song goes down, where does it begin?
C: High.
    And start over here. (Indicates left edge of board.)
T: Fine, Andrew. Write it as we sing.

C:

          — —
              — —
                  — —
                      — —
                          — —
                            — —
                              ——
                                  ——

    Now it's right.
    The Little Man has more lines, too; four on each step.
T: Does it? Try it and see. Be sure to sing as you write.
    Everyone should show it in the air as Andrew writes. ——— Are there
    four on each step?
C: Five on the first and three on the last.

The children's responses will determine the complexity and pacing of sessions in writing line notation. At all times, the teacher has the responsibility of defining the challenge—"Let's try just this part." He must be sure there is a musical experience to represent: "Sing and show the melody with your hand; how did your hand move? Step the rhythm; clap the rhythm. Can you say the *long*'s and *short*'s?"

The one who is writing must actually walk from left to right as he represents the contour of the melody. The line notation is in this way a visual translation of the performer's body movement, with the left to right spacing showing the time dimension. Distinctive fragments of the song repertoire may be notated at first as a group project. Everyone, including the writer, sings. If the line picture is wrong or ambiguous, the teacher may sing it to help the child find the error. Shapes that occur in more than one song encourage further exploration.

T: What song begins like this?

           ——   ——

C: *Ritsch Ratsch.*
    Wake Me!

T: Both! There are others, too. But for now, if I want this to be *Wake Me!*
    how can I be sure you will know. Let's sing it.

C: I'll play the drum in the empty places. —————

T: Can you show that on the board?

C:

C: I like the sound of the triangle. Play the triangle.

T: Then make a picture that will tell us to play it.

C:

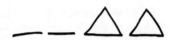

T: Good!

C: *Ritsch Ratsch* doesn't have empty spaces for playing.

T: What does it have?

C: It has "bom bom bom's."

T: Shall we show those? John, you try. We'll sing the whole first part;
    you write just the "bom's."

C:

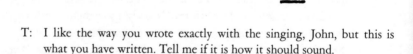

T: I like the way you wrote exactly with the singing, John, but this is
    what you have written. Tell me if it is how it should sound.

C: You made a mistake at the end.
    It does go up there; I remember my hand went up.

T: Then what is wrong? John, can you play the last group on the piano?
    Start here. (Indicates middle C.) We'll help you by singing it.

C:

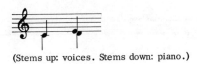

(Stems up: voices. Stems down: piano.)

That one's wrong.

T: Try another.

C:

Wrong again.

T: It can't be that one because we know it goes up. Try again.

C:

T: Almost!

C:

That's it!
It skips over keys.

T: You're right. How shall we show that on the board?

C: Make bigger spaces.

_____

_____

_____

T: Very good. Richard, remember your song? How do the "bumps" go? Sing it.

C:

We're rid-ing on the bus,   bump,   bump,   bump.

They skip over, going down.
T: Please show it on the board.

Conventional Notation

Teachers should be warned against introducing conventional notation before line notation has musical meaning for the children. All too often the busy work of naming notes and drawing clefs has little to do with actual musical experience.

Children need many opportunities to compare examples of melodic stepping and skipping by singing, by designing in space and on the chalkboard, and by playing on the piano or melody bells. Then they can proceed to identification of single examples, for which they refer to kinesthetic, aural, and visual images of their experiences. The teacher who asks "How could you tell?" can often gain insights into the child's concept-formation process. Children must understand that melodies go up or down, and they can step or skip, before they are introduced to conventional notation.

T: Remember yesterday when we sang so many songs and made the line pictures? I left one on the board.

Who can tell what it is?
C: It's *Hot Cross Buns.*
It's Richard's "bumps."
You can't tell if it steps or skips over.

T: You're right. Unless we have both pictures so we can compare them, we can't be sure. But there is a way of writing music so you *can* tell. I promised Elliott I would show him how. Would all of you like to see?

C: I saw it in my sister's music book.

T: You did? Did you see some lines like this?

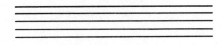

C: Yes, and big dots and other marks, too.

T: We'll get to that. First, I wonder who could tell me something about the walkway to our back door?

C: It's cement.

T: And what did we notice when we played hop-scotch on it?

C: It has lines.

T: I'm going to draw the same kind of sidewalk on the floor with chalk.

C: Sometimes I step on all the lines on the sidewalk.
   I like to hop over the lines.

T: On my chalk sidewalk I'm going to step on a line, then in a space, on a line, in a space. Watch me. ——— Can you do that? Try it, Marisol.

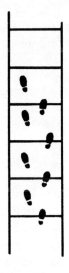

You try it, Abraham, and say where you're stepping. ——— (Every-one has a turn.) Now let's go back to the lines for music. How many lines do I have? Let's count them from the bottom up.

C: One, two, three, four, five.

T: How many spaces are between the lines? Let's count those from the bottom up, too.

C: One, two, three, four.

T: This is called a *staff*. It has five lines with four spaces in between. Now see what I can do with this circle of cardboard; we can call it a music *note*. I'm going to help it walk on the staff. I put it on a line, in a space, on a line, in a space.

C: Just the way we walked on the sidewalk.

T: Exactly. If I start here (first line) and go here (first space), then here (second line), which direction am I going on the board?

C: Up.

T: What song do you know that goes up?

C: *The Little Man.*

T: Let's sing it! Watch the note! ———

C: Sing *Jack and Jill.*

T: All right, we will. Watch the note! ——— What song is this? (Shows descending scale.)

C: Jack and Jill coming down.

T: Fine! I'll do it again and we can sing it. ——— How about this one? ("Plays" *Hot Cross Buns.* On "One-a-penny, two-a-penny" lifts note slightly and replaces it in proper rhythm. Children sing as they recognize the song.)

Teachers of young children realize the need to be clear and precise in their explanations and directions. The placing of a note "on a line" presents a problem: the common interpretation of *on* is indeed *on top of,* as in "on the table." The "sidewalk" experience makes clear the music notation use of *on a line.* The transfer to the board for staff notation permits the exact reenactment of the *up*'s and *down*'s of melody designed in space. (Speaking of the *top* and *bottom* of the board in discussions of *high* and *low* facilitates children's understanding of directions when they began to write on paper.) Returning to the "sidewalk," one easily discovers that he goes from line to line or space to space as he lunges or leaps over the intervening positions.

There are several ways to notate a song or fragment quickly and legibly, and yet have the notation easy to change. A staff can be painted on one part of the chalkboard; notes drawn with chalk can then be erased without disturbing the staff. Short diagonal lines as notes show positions easily. For "fatter" notes, use the side of a short piece of chalk.

Magnetic disks (on a slate chalkboard) designed for math work are convenient notes for a staff drawn to size. The spaces should accommodate the disks easily.

For flashcards, a felt pen makes the staff. Gummed circles, commercially available, can be notes.

T: What song is this? (Writes on staff.)

C: *Hot Cross Buns.*
T: Let's sing and follow the notes. The notes are—
C: On a line, in a space, on a line.
T: Is that how Richard's "bumps" come down?
C: His has bigger spaces.
　　It skips over a key on the piano.
T: Yes. Stepping is line, space, line, space, line.
　　(Writes notes on staff.)

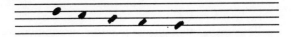

Sing it with me.

line　space　line　space　line

If we start Richard's "bumps" here (indicates fourth line) what will you skip over?
C: This one. (Indicates note in third space.)
T: We'll erase it, then.
C: Erase the other space note too.

T: Good! Point to the notes as we sing.

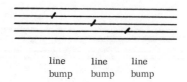

line   line   line
bump   bump   bump

If we put the space notes back, we sing,

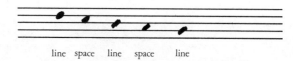

line space line space line

Let's sing first the stepping one, then the skipping one, and watch the notes. ———— Who can write the skipping one if it starts with a note in the third space?

C:

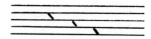

T: What words will you sing?
C:

Space   space   space

Following and singing along with a moving note cardboard or magnetic disk is a profitable activity. It encourages complete attention and involvement. This kind of music reading emphasizes the ongoing quality of the music. The teacher can tailor the challenge easily, starting with familiar songs or fragments and patterns on parts of a scale. Eventually he can teach parts of a new song in this way. The children sing the fragments with "la's" at first, then with words.

Writing on the staff without a clef permits practice with different positions, starting sometimes on a line, sometimes in a space. Key signatures are not needed. The focus is on the shape of the melody. The general directive to start low if the song goes up, and so on, will obviate the use of added (leger) lines.

Children who make up songs are highly motivated to write them in conventional notation. A logical progression is to design the melody in the air, use line notation, discuss the location of steps versus skips, and finally, write on the staff.

"Research" into songbooks by the children should be encouraged. They can be guided to discover how note stems are made: if the note is high on the staff, the stem starts on the left edge of the note head and comes down. If it is low, the stem is on the right and goes up.

Note values can be introduced as a convenient way to show the rela tive length of tones. The discussion should always be related to familiar music experiences.

C: I wrote *Hot Cross Buns.*

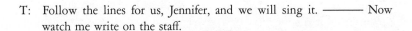

T: Follow the lines for us, Jennifer, and we will sing it. ——— Now watch me write on the staff.

C: That's *Hot Cross Buns,* too.
T: Yes, Shelley. Help us follow the notes as we sing.
C: The empty ones are the buns.
    They're the long ones.
T: You're right. They're called *half* notes and the black ones are *quarter* notes.
C: (Pointing to eighth notes.) Why do those have lines joining them?
T: Why do you think? How does that part look in the line picture?
C: They're much shorter.
T: Everyone clap the beat with me. (Starts a moderate beat.) Now let's sing the song and notice where you clap. I'll mark the claps under the notes.

C: Two notes go to one clap in that place.

Jo - sie   Jo - sie   Jo - sie   Jo - sie

T: Very good. Those are called *eighth* notes. They're joined together to show they go to one beat or clap. Did you notice the claps for the half notes—the empty ones?
C: They got two claps.
The "hot" and the "cross" each got one clap.
T: Absolutely right. If we clap once for each quarter note, each half note gets two claps.

CONCLUSION

Young children are usually fascinated with developing their verbal skills. Those who have experienced the expressive qualities of music through body movement and singing are naturally excited about reading and writing its symbols. Viable experiences in notation can provide opportunities to emphasize to them that, in every case, the symbol stands for the doing, the real thing. Unfortunately, it is often the teacher who is easily sidetracked; the child's ability to write and identify symbols is allowed to become an end in itself, perhaps because it produces a (visible) product, easy to evaluate.

Material for developing notation skills includes not only the song repertoire, but the children's improvisation on the piano or melody bells. Rhythmic patterns for nonpitched percussion supply a different challenge. Flashcards can be extended to poster-size copies of short songs. When the child is challenged to find a familiar example in the teacher's music book, a whole new world is opened to him. Some children are curious about unfamiliar signs. Explanations should be limited to the symbols that are relevant to their experience, and always in terms of the musical content. Definitions should be avoided.

If the child is eager to write music, it is essential that he be required to "sing and design," "sing and play" after as well as before he writes; the direct connection between sound and symbol cannot be overemphasized. When these efforts are integrated with reading printed music, the child realizes his power to operate independently, a proud achievement of adult behavior. He can study the sounds of music in a special way when the notes are before him. Symbolic representations can indeed be an important phase of the child's cognitive and affective musical growth.

VII
EVALUATION OF MUSIC LEARNING

The teacher needs to know the kind and extent of individual children's music learning as it is taking place in the classroom. This information is essential to the planning of purposeful activities. However, the teacher's observations may not yield this data directly. The teacher, perhaps guilty of wishful thinking, is easily misled by an eager look or a rote answer prompted by the child's sensitivity to his expectation. The child may suppress his different answer or lack of understanding in response to inadvertent cues given by the teacher, whom he wants to please.

Formulation of long-range objectives, carefully designated as to nature—affective or cognitive, and in the latter case, whether concept, skill, or knowledge of repertoire or terms—give focus to the teacher's on-going evaluation of learning as well as direction to his total program. Expressing these objectives in terms of student behavior and planning ways of evaluating their achievement is a challenging task. The objectives must take into account the broad rationale for music learning as well as the children's previous experience. They will be directly subject to the teacher's skills and style plus limitations of time and physical facilities.

AFFECTIVE OBJECTIVES

Affective behavior, by its very nature, is not amenable to precise measurement. The following checklist for classroom observation may give a general picture of the child's attitudes toward music experiences. Individual children's actions may suggest other meaningful behaviors. The teacher will want to evolve his own list. The important role of music learning in the child's total development should be the basis of the teacher's criteria for desirable attitudes.

CLASSROOM OBSERVATION OF AFFECTIVE BEHAVIOR

_____

Child's name

Enter the date of when you observe minimum response; the degree of proficiency is not crucial to the evaluation of attitudes.

1. Volunteers appropriate movements for action songs:

    _____

2. Volunteers novel movements for action songs:

    _____

3. Responds independently in listening-moving games:

    _____

4. Joins in group singing without "invitation";

    _____

5. Sings alone when asked during the regular music activities:

    _____

6. Chooses instrument playing and listening during free play:

    _____

7. Sings independently during other activities:

    _____

COGNITIVE OBJECTIVES

In this sample list of objectives, the emphasis is deliberately on music concept-formation rather than on skills and repertoire *per se*. This is not to underestimate the social and personal values of performance, the enjoyment and intrinsic motivation it provides. Rather it is to underscore that added benefits can be derived from these activities when they are built on understanding.

At the end of a first year of purposive music-movement activities, most young children should be able to:

MOVE

1. Respond through body movement to marches, lullabies, and descriptive selections, showing obvious climax points.
2. Respond accurately in action songs and singing games.
3. Respond in movement to the beat, meter, and phrasing of music of elementary design.
4. Design the melodic contour of simple phrases, using hand levels and body movement, distinguishing between *up, down,* and *on a level.*

PLAY

5. Play the pulse in ensemble with songs and instrumental selections on nonpitched percussion instruments.
6. Play (echo) short rhythmic patterns and phrases by ear on nonpitched percussion.
7. Play the piano or melody bells to show *up, down,* and *on a level.*

SING

8. Sing a variety of appropriate folk and holiday songs, giving attention to mood, diction, and dynamics.
9. Sing (echo) short melodic patterns by ear.

IMPROVISE

10. Improvise rhythmic patterns, using classroom instruments or clapping.
11. Improvise melodic shapes, singing.

VERBALIZE CONCEPTS

12. Distinguish between repetition (*same*) and obvious contrast (*different*) of phrases.
13. Recognize classroom instruments by sound, singly and in combinations.

14. Identify obvious contrasts in dynamics, agogics, and tone quality as expressive qualities of music heard.
    a. *Loud, soft.*
    b. *Fast, slow.*
    c. *Smooth, jumpy.*
15. Identify *up, down,* and *on a level* in melodic shapes.
16. Identify *short* and *long* in rhythmic patterns.

INDIVIDUAL PERFORMANCE TESTS

Formal testing of individual children may not be feasible or even desirable in every school situation. The tests are included here for the added dimension they may afford to the formulation of objectives. In addition, they may suggest modes of informal evaluation.

If used as a measuring tool in an extended curriculum study, the tests will necessarily be adjusted to conform with the objectives of the particular year of activities. The teacher should be familiar with the testing procedure and scoring sheets so that he can focus on enjoying the music activities with the child. Although the use of prerecorded music would permit exactly uniform stimulus situations for each child, it would not allow adjusting to the child's singing range and his natural walking tempo.

Preliminary portions (in italics) should not be scored.
(—) cannot   (+) can

FOLLOW THE MUSIC

"Show how you walked to school this morning."
    Pick up the child's tempo, accompanying him with improvised music at the piano.
"Follow the music; do what it tells you to do."
    Interrupt several times without warning, then proceed in the same tempo.
"Show the music as it gets louder and softer."
    Exaggerate the shadings, from pianissimo to fortissimo in eight beats.
"Here is some walking music. It may get louder and softer. Do what it tells you to do."

Play in the child's tempo, $\frac{4}{4}$, five two-measure phrases with the following dynamics:

1. *mf*
2. *mf*
3. **pp** to *ff*
4. *ff* to **pp**
5. **pp** to *ff*

Do not score on the decrescendo. This requires more control than should be expected of a young child.

    a. Maintains steady beat   (−) (+)

    b. Indicates crescendo by
       gradual increase in
       energy of movement.   (−) (+)

RHYTHMIC PATTERN

"Let your feet follow this music."

"Now, follow this."

"You stepped *short* and *long* sounds."
"What kind are these?"

    a. Identifies *long*.   (−) (+)

"What kind are these?"

    b. Identifies *short*.   (−) (+)

"Listen to this pattern; step it."

    c. Steps pattern   (−) (+)

"Step the pattern some more; say the long's and short's as you step."

           d.   Identifies *long's* and *short's*.   (−) (+)

PLAYING FOR MOVEMENT

    The teacher walks (in the child's tempo) and sings "Let's Go Walking."

"Play for my walking with the rhythm sticks."

           a.   Maintains steady beat.   (−) (+)

"Now I will be a big bell."

    Teacher swings while singing "Oh, How Lovely Is the Evening."

"Play for my swinging on the triangle."

           b.   Maintains steady first beats.   (−) (+)

HIGH AND LOW

"I will sing some tones for you.

"If you hear a high tone, reach high with your hands.

"If you hear a low tone, reach low with your hands."

    Teacher sings:

        a.   Responds *high*.   (−) (+)
        b.   Responds *low*.   (−) (+)
        c.   Responds *low*.   (−) (+)
        d.   Responds *high*.   (−) (+)

UP, DOWN, AND ON A LEVEL

"Listen to the melody. It will go *up* or *down* or it will stay *on a level*.

"Now sing it with me.

"Let's sing it once more; this time, show the direction of the melody with your hand."

Do not mark on accuracy of singing.

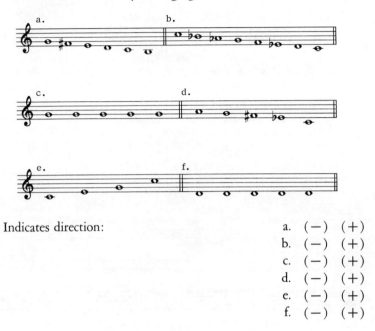

Indicates direction:

a. (−) (+)
b. (−) (+)
c. (−) (+)
d. (−) (+)
e. (−) (+)
f. (−) (+)

ECHOING RHYTHMIC PATTERNS (CLAPPING)

"I will clap a pattern for you; when I point to you, clap the same pattern back to me. Always wait until I point to you."

Memorize the patterns so that eye contact with the child is maintained, the test being a "conversation." Clap musically, shading in accordance with the rhythmic shape. If the child misses a pattern, mark (−) but repeat the measure until the beat and meter are re-established.

a.   a. (−) (+)

b.   b. (−) (+)

c.   c. (−) (+)

d.   d. (−) (+)

e.   e. (−) (+)

f.   f. (−) (+)

g.   g. (−) (+)

h.   h. (−) (+)

ECHOING MELODIC PATTERNS (SINGING)

Match single tones to find proper range.

a. (−) (+)
b. (−) (+)
c. (−) (+)
d. (−) (+)
e. (−) (+)
f. (−) (+)
g. (−) (+)
h. (−) (+)
i. (−) (+)

j. (−) (+)
k. (−) (+)

METER

"Show how a very big bell swings; be the biggest bell you can."

Pick up the child's tempo, treating each swing as a dotted half note. Improvise in 3/4, using measures of

$$ \text{♩., ♩ ♩, ♩ ♩ ♩} $$

    a. Moves with first beats.   (−) (+)
    b. Maintains smoothness of movement. (−) (+)

AGOGICS

"Pretend you are a train, standing in the station; the music will tell you when to start, and just how to go—faster and slower."

Adagio to allegro to adagio.
Repeat to score.

        a. Follows accelerando.   (−) (+)
        b. Follows ritardando.   (−) (+)

PLAYING MELODIC PATTERNS BY EAR

"This will be our starting place."

Indicate "E" above "middle C" on piano or melody bells.

"I will sing a melody for you."

"Sing it with me."

"Sing it again and show the *up, down,* and *level* with your hand."

"Now start here and play the melody as you sing."

    Designates "E."

    Follow this procedure with each melody.

a. (−) (+)
b. (−) (+)
c. (−) (+)
d. (−) (+)
e. (−) (+)

IMPROVISING RHYTHMIC PATTERNS (CLAPPING)

"Make up a rhythm for me to echo."
       Child's rhythm:
          a. Demonstrates idea of coherency.   (−) (+)
"Clap another rhythm; clap it over and over again."
       Child's rhythm:
          b. Demonstrates idea of coherency.   (−) (+)
          c. Repeats accurately.   (−) (+)

IMPROVISING MELODIC PATTERNS (SINGING)

"Make up a little melody for me to echo."
    Child's melody:

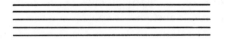

          a. Demonstrates idea of shape   (−) (+)
"Sing another melody; sing it over and over again."
    Child's melody:

b. Demonstrates idea of shape.	$(-)$ $(+)$
c. Repeats accurately.	$(-)$ $(+)$

TONE QUALITY OF INSTRUMENTS

Two short phrases of each are prerecorded on tape. Display the instruments.

"Point to the instrument(s) that is (are) sounding and tell the name of each."

	Recognizes		Names	
Triangle	a. $(-)$ $(+)$	l. $(-)$ $(+)$		
Drum	b. $(-)$ $(+)$	m. $(-)$ $(+)$		
Rhythm sticks	c. $(-)$ $(+)$	n. $(-)$ $(+)$		
Tambourine	d. $(-)$ $(+)$	o. $(-)$ $(+)$		
Piano	e. $(-)$ $(+)$	p. $(-)$ $(+)$		
Jingle bells	f. $(-)$ $(+)$	q. $(-)$ $(+)$		
Violin	g. $(-)$ $(+)$	r. $(-)$ $(+)$		
Recorder	h. $(-)$ $(+)$	s. $(-)$ $(+)$		
Triangle and Drum	i. $(-)$ $(+)$	t. $(-)$ $(+)$		
Piano and Recorder	j. $(-)$ $(+)$	u. $(-)$ $(+)$		
Drum and Violin	k. $(-)$ $(+)$	v. $(-)$ $(+)$		

DYNAMICS

"Listen."

Sing pianissimo:

"Now listen again:
Repeat fortissimo.
"Did they sound the same?"

a. Discriminates.	$(-)$ $(+)$

"How was the last one different?"

b. Identifies louder.	$(-)$ $(+)$

"Listen."

Sing fortissimo:

"Now listen again."
    Repeat pianissimo.
"Did they sound the same?"
        c. Discriminates.   (−) (+)
"How was the last one different?"
        d. Identifies softer.   (−) (+)

TEMPO

"Listen."
    Sing adagio:

"Now listen again":
    Repeat allegro.
"Did they sound the same?"
        a. Discriminates.   (−) (+)
"How was the last one different?"
        b. Identifies faster.   (−) (+)
"Listen."
    Sing allegro:

"Now listen again."
    Repeat adagio.
"Did they sound the same?"
        c. Discriminates.   (−) (+)
"How was the last one different?"
        d. Identifies slower.   (−) (+)

"In the song 'If You're Happy and You Know It' you have the chance to decide how you will show it. Sing the song and do what the words tell you."

a.	Maintains melody.	(−)	(+)
b.	Articulates main words.	(−)	(+)
c.	Indicates appropriate action or accompaniment.	(−)	(+)

"Sing 'Hello, Somebody.' Decide where the garden gate is. Knock only when the song tells you to."

d.	Maintains melody	(−)	(+)
e.	Articulates main words.	(−)	(+)
f.	Phrases accurately.	(−)	(+)

VIII
CONCLUSION

This book has considered the theory and practice of purposive music experiences for young children; it has emphasized the exploration and discovery of musical concepts and attitudes through direct sensory involvement. The basic structure of music has been defined in terms of (1) concepts *of* music; (2) concepts *about* music; and (3) minimal skills and repertoire. We have suggested that cognitive and affective musical learning can be facilitated by exploiting the valid relationship of movement to music. Music experiences of participation and perception beginning in the child's life-space have been described as the means of his intellectual and emotional growth.

The focus has been music learning. However, the application to comprehensive educational goals is implicit: the same basic listening skills and response controls are crucial to learning in other subject areas as well. The child's direct (*enactive* and *iconic*) experiences, planned to lay the foundation of the structure of music, also feed into concept formation and skills in science, social studies, and especially language. His identification of feelings and values in music activities when he responds with his body and his voice nurture emotional growth with important ramifications for special concerns of early childhood educators. These include work with the emotionally-disturbed, the brain-damaged, and the culturally-deprived. There are exciting possibilities of using this approach in special remedial projects; the more musically sensitive the experiences, the more dramatic the gains in these areas are likely to be.[1]

There is an urgent need to make relevant research findings on human

---

[1] Some early childhood specialists who corroborate this statement are Adele Davidson, Early Childhood Coordinator, District I, New York City Public Schools; Jeannette Vosk, Head Psychologist, Pre-School Child Development Program, New York City Public Schools; Irene Krull, Program Designer, Headstart and Follow Through, New York, N.Y. and Atlanta, Ga.

performance available to the teacher, to bridge the gap between research and practice. Calvin Taylor suggests that "educational engineers" are needed for a complete research and development program in education. Music educators recognize another gap that needs closing. It is the one between the discipline content—what music is all about—and the classroom teacher's often limited concept of its nature and general availability. Performers and composers may be blamed in some measure for capitalizing on the romantic mystique of "musical talent" to intimidate the lay person.

Although the writer's concern is with the crucial need to bridge these gaps, delegation of the task to "engineers" carries the risk of developing new jargon and pat methodologies with limited long-range benefits. The challenge should be rather for responsible teachers to reach out to other fields for help in establishing more viable bases for their own work. For the early-childhood teacher, this means constant examining of his own attitudes toward music, and widening of his esthetic horizons; searching for new insights into children's behavior, from psychological research and other subject-area studies; questioning of the real objectives of music methodologies; and becoming ever more aware of the exciting educational potentials of the interaction between the child and music.

APPENDIX

THE EURYTHMICS OF
ÉMILE JAQUES-DALCROZE

To my mind, musical education should be entirely based on hearing or, at any
rate, on the perception of musical phenomena: The ear gradually accustoming itself
to grasp the relations between notes, keys, and chords, and the whole body, by
means of special exercises, initiating itself into the appreciation of rhythmic,
dynamic, and agogic nuances of music.[1]

Musicality is a complicated and elusive concept. Émile Jaques-Dalcroze
pioneered in approaching it; he found ways of experiencing musical
phenomena in many contexts and from many vantage points, by physical experience of the separate elements of music. He discovered how to
help others to abstract the elements and thereby to analyze the content
and mechanisms of musical expression through body movement—for
purposes of musicality.

The attributes and educational value of Dalcroze Eurythmics are not
always clear to those who have only read of it. Some Dalcroze propo-
nents claim the work must be personally experienced to be appreciated.
Certainly there seem to be no articulate, reasonably brief descriptions
available. This attempt at definition is considered in the context of current educational thinking; it is based on the writer's learning from outstanding teachers who worked with M. Jaques at different periods[2] and
on discussion with Dalcroze colleagues.

Understanding music means being able to make one's own order of
its sounds. This understanding, whether in hearing, singing, playing, or
"making-up" can be facilitated by drawing upon one's movement experience of time, space, and energy.[3] (The use of the movement experi-

---

[1] Émile Jaques-Dalcroze, *Rhythm, Music and Education,* New York; G. P. Putnam's Sons, 1921, p. 109
[2] Nelly Reuschel, Hilda Schuster, Paul Boepple, and John Colman.
[3] "Music is significant for us as human beings principally because it embodies movement of a specifically
human type that goes to the roots of our being and takes shape in the inner gestures which embody our deepest and most intimate responses." Roger Sessions, *The Musical Experience of Composer, Performer, Listener,* New
York: Atheneum, 1965, p. 18.

ence may be quite unconscious.) The musical result is a function of the quantity and quality of one's movement experiences and the freedom and technique available to each person for making use of this resource. In Bruner's terms, it is the use of the *enactive* and *iconic* modes and the translation from one to the other, in both directions. This is what Dalcroze Eurythmics is all about.

Émile Jaques-Dalcroze, as a Harmony professor at the Geneva Conservatory at the turn of the century, questioned the prevalent supposition that musical responsiveness was an innate characteristic. Moreover, he rejected the traditional theoretical approach in vogue; it could be pursued "successfully" by the student without affective involvement and without even hearing the musical content of the exercises. Dalcroze realized the possibility of having his students refine their aural imagery from stored experiences and symbols (he called this "inner hearing") and of singing some aspects of the images for examination and organization. He recognized the role of spontaneity (natural feeling, temperament) in this procedure and its connection, in turn, with physical action.

Dalcroze had studied with Mathis Lussy; he acknowledged his debt to Lussy for "a brilliant system of analyzing and explaining musical rhythm and expression."[4] Specifically he learned from him "that everything in music can be related to fundamental physiological laws; how each nuance, each accent has its *raison-d'être;* and how, finally, a melodic phrase, with its expressive and rhythmic interpretation, formes an organic entity and how intimately it is related to its harmonization."[5]

Treating rhythm, with its roots in physical movement, as the organizer of musical elements, Dalcroze thought of using the body as a "musical instrument" for personal, physical experience of these elements in their dynamic relationship. He began by helping his students relate their normal, even walk to the same on-going pulse in instrumental or vocal performance. Dalcroze improvised music at the piano to vivify the student's feeling for the pulse.

Out of his experimentation and experience, some basic principles evolved. Dalcroze proclaimed "Rhythm is movement," "Rhythm insures the completeness of life's manifestations." He conceived the ideal

[4] Émile Jaques-Dalcroze, *Rhythm, Music and Education.* New York: G. P. Putnam's Sons, 1921, p. 54.
[5] Dalcroze.

education to be accessible through Eurythmics, which he called "education for and through rhythm." These grandiose statements are properly understood in context: Dalcroze was vehemently denouncing the unmusical educational practices in vogue in the early part of the century. The principles of Eurythmics as developed by Dalcroze and as practiced (ideally) by his followers may be more precisely stated:

1. The time-space-energy relationship of body movement has a counterpart in musical expression, in which thought and feeling are inextricably related.

2. Musicality can be encouraged by consciously using one's own body movement in conjunction with the keenest aural perception and imagery ("inner hearing").

3. Joyous and satisfying experiences may be devised to facilitate this correlation, leading in turn to increased sensitivity and skill in manipulating the elements of music.

Dalcroze invented musical exercises with improvised music. They may be called games because, in addition to objectives of physical and intellectual training and improvement, they have some characteristics of contests. In each game, the individual student plays "against" the music, according to set rules. The motivation is recreation, without the threats involved in right/wrong tasks or student against student competition.

The student playing the games is challenged to respond not only accurately, but with sensitivity to the expressive continuity of the music. Complete attention and concentration on the sounds heard encourage the development of the body's freedom to respond directly, without extraneous muscular movements (inhibiting tensions or mannerisms). The games may be classified:

1. *Follow.* The student steps to the beat or the pattern of improvised music, following gradual changes of dynamics, agogics, and touch.

2. *Quick Response.* The student responds overtly in a prearranged way to a stimulus signal, which may be a rhythmic, harmonic, or melodic detail in the improvised music, or a verbal command. He must integrate his response into the musical flow.

3. *Interrupted Canon.* The teacher improvises in consistent meter (or some transformation of it) with varying rhythmic patterns, interspersing full measure rests after each measure of music. During the

rest, the student steps the pattern he has just heard, reproducing the same dynamics and nuance.

4. *Canon.* The teacher improvises in consistent meter (or some transformation of it) with varying rhythmic patterns. After a prearranged interval of time, usually one measure, the student steps to the music as played, with or without conducting.

Coordination of cognitive and physical actions is the first step of a given activity in the Eurythmics class, but it is only a means to an end. The objectives of developing the physical skills for realizing certain "intellectualized" musical devices with the body must be understood: by experiencing the juxtaposition of the musical elements kinesthetically, the student can discover and come to understand musical ideas in terms of their potential expressive use. He acquires in this way a storehouse of aural and kinesthetic images, and then uses them for achieving concepts, as a repertoire for sensitive performance and hearing, and as a vocabulary for improvisation and composition. Thus, Dalcroze Eurythmics is a means toward keener perception and response; it is in no sense an independent art medium.

The study techniques of Eurythmics devised by Dalcroze[6] are flexible to class needs:

1. *Rhythmic Patterns.* Step the durations of rhythmic patterns played repeatedly within a changing melodic/harmonic context. Even or uneven beats and measures may be featured.

2. *Conducting.* Conduct the meter, using enlarged, stylized conductor's beats. When the student can do this automatically, he has a useful "built-in" device for analyzing the rhythmic patterns heard and subsequently stepped.

3. *Swings.* Swing the body, arms following, in various meters; use with stepped patterns.

4. *Augmentation; Diminution.* Modify a pattern by stepping it two or three times as fast or as slow. The conducting may remain the same, or change with the pattern.

5. *Rests.* Change patterns by adding rests or by substituting rests for notes. The dynamic quality of the rests can be experienced in movement.

---

[6] These descriptions are not all-inclusive; they should, however, indicate the variety of learning strategies that can be invented.

6. *Syncopation.* Inhibit or excite portions of a pattern with rests, ties, or dynamic accents.

7. *Accents.* Shift the metric accent to different positions in a given pattern.

8. *Transformation.* Shift the grouping of subdivisions within the measure.

Example: 3/4 to 6/8.

9. *Polymeter.* Experience (clapping and stepping) different groupings simultaneously. In slow tempi the combined rhythm is analyzed.

Example: 4 against 3.

In fast tempi the established locomotion speed facilitates the coordination, the ease in feeling the total unit subdivided.

10. *Complementary Rhythm.* Step the "negative" of a pattern, in various note values.

Example:

The pattern:

(Dalcroze used the actual note value of the beat in place of the bottom figure of the time signature. This is especially useful in compound time.)

Complementary rhythm in ♩ 's:

Complementary rhythm in ♪ 's:

11. *Polyrhythm.* Perform two patterns simultaneously.

Example:

Clap:

Step:

12. *Phrasing.* Experience the phrasing by change of direction, arm gestures, or repeated use of one foot. (Stamp, tap, or glide on the last tone of the phrase; use the same foot to begin the next phrase.)

13. *Anacrusis; Metacrusis.* Identify the *crusis* (climax) of the measure; manipulate the anacrusis or the metacrusis by augmentation, diminution, adding or substituting rests, adding or subtracting notes.

14. *Plastique Animé.* Akin to a young child's "dancing" to music he hears, this free movement is often misunderstood by spectators. It is not dance, but a conscious exploration of movement in response to a given musical task. The result may resemble dancing, but its objective makes the difference: it is specifically to show that the student has heard and understood the music. Composed music is sometimes used, and the class may respond individually or as a group. Any of the study techniques may be integrated into improvisation assignments; time, space, and energy are the materials of these creative samples.

The Dalcroze approach is notable in its contribution to its student's rhythmic awareness, vitality, and freedom. Two examples may be singled out:

1. The expressive potential of a phrase may be analyzed in terms of its anacrusis, crusis and metacrusis.

2. Uneven beats and measures can significantly enlarge the musical vocabulary. Dalcroze made a unique contribution to the understanding and manipulation of these additive rhythms. They are based on the *chronos protos,* the smallest indivisible value of ancient Greek theory, also found in Arabian and Indian music and in Gregorian chant. After studying such rhythms through body movement, it is understandable that their notation as syncopations in regular meter is misleading to the performer, and in turn, to the listener.

Viewed in retrospect, Jaques-Dalcroze's objectives were always toward dual growth—cognitive and affective—through music. He argued vehemently for giving students opportunities for perceiving and responding, and with seemingly unlimited resources, planned learning experiences in which musical materials were experienced before they were analyzed and notated. And when the symbols were meaningful, he encouraged their manipulation to expand the musical repertoire.

The student's natural walk, an easily maintained even beat, was the starting point. By providing musical accompaniment, the freedom to move was encouraged, and the dynamic flow of the music was in turn highlighted. From the very beginning, as Dalcroze emphasized the interrelatedness of time, space, and energy in movement, these considerations became the means of focusing on the expressive potential of the musical elements in synthesis.

The rationale for Eurythmics is eminently clear in contemporary psychological findings. Although much is still unknown of the mental process of learning, certain aspects of perception and adaptation that cause changes in behavior are increasingly understood. In this regard, Richard Held's research shows that the muscles and motor parts of the individual's nervous system must be involved. The adaptation is not just a change in processing of incoming data from the eyes and the ears; the information must be drawn from the child's contact with the environment. This learning phenomenon, called *reafference,* clarifies how learning can result from the student's physical enactment of the ongoing stimulus. Reafference permits him to discover the attributes of the music through his own kinesthetic sense. This translation between the *enactive* and *iconic* ways of knowing is the basis of Émile Jaques-Dalcroze's musical and educational rationale and his methodology.

BIBLIOGRAPHY

Almy, Millie. *Ways of Studying Children.* From Materials Prepared by Ruth Cunningham and Associates. New York: Bureau of Publications, Teachers College, 1959.

————. "Wishful Thinking about Children's Thinking?" *Teachers College Record,* **62,** 396–406, February 1961.

————. "Young Children's Thinking about Natural Phenomena." Horace Mann-Lincoln Institute of School Experimentation Interim Report. New York: Teachers College, Columbia University, 1960. Mimeographed.

Anderson, Richard C. "Introduction to Part III." David P. Ausubel and Richard C. Anderson, eds. *Readings in the Psychology of Cognition.* New York: Holt, Rinehart and Winston, 1965, pp. 395–405.

Apel, Willi. *Harvard Dictionary of Music.* Cambridge, Mass.: Harvard University Press, 1964.

Arnheim, Rudolf. "Expression." Morris Philipson, ed. *Aesthetics Today.* Meridian Book. Cleveland: World Publishing, 1961, pp. 188–207.

————. "Gestalt Psychology and Artistic Form." Lancelot Law Whyte, ed. *Aspects of Form.* Bloomington: Indiana University Press, 1961, pp. 196–208.

————. *Toward a Psychology of Art.* Berkeley, University of California Press, 1966.

Ashton-Warner, Sylvia. *Teacher.* New York: Bantam Books, 1964.

Association for Supervision and Curriculum Development. *Intellectual Development: Another Look.* Papers from the ASCD Eighth Curriculum Research Institute. A. Harry Passow and Robert R. Leeper, eds. Washington: The Association, 1964.

————. *Learning and Mental Health in the School.* 1966 Yearbook. Walter B. Waetjen and Robert R. Leeper, eds. Washington: The Association, 1966.

Ausubel, David P. "Learning by Discovery: Rationale and Mystique." National Association of Secondary School Principals. *Bulletin,* **45,** 18–58, December 1961.

————. "Some Psychological and Educational Limitations of Learning by Discovery." *The Arithmetic Teacher,* 11, 290–302, May 1964.

————. "A Teaching Strategy for Culturally Deprived Pupils: Cognitive and Motivational Considerations." *The School Review,* 71, 454–461, Winter 1963.

Beardsley, Monroe. *Aesthetics: Problems in the Philosophy of Criticism.* New York: Harcourt, Brace & World, 1958.

Bereiter, Carl and Siegfried Englemann. *Teaching Disadvantaged Children in the Pre-School.* Englewood Cliffs, N. J.: Prentice-Hall, 1967. [Sanction of Bereiter's methodology is not intended.]

Bloom, Benjamin S. *Stability and Change in Human Characteristics.* New York: John Wiley and Sons, 1964.

Bloom, Benjamin S. and others. *Taxonomy of Educational Objectives, The Classification of Educational Goals, Handbook I: Cognitive Domain.* New York: David McKay, 1956.

————. *Taxonomy of Educational Objectives, The Classification of Educational Goals, Handbook II: Affective Domain.* New York: David McKay, 1964.

Blount, Bernice S. "Assisting Young Children to Transfer from Auditory Language Signals to Visual Language Signals in the Reading Process." Doctor of Education Project Report, New York: Teachers College, Columbia University, 1966. Typewritten.

Bruner, Jerome S. "The Course of Cognitive Growth." *American Psychologist,* 19, 1–15, January 1964.

————. *On Knowing: Essays for the Left Hand.* Cambridge, Mass.: Belknap Press of Harvard University Press, 1962.

————. *The Process of Education.* First Vintage Edition. New York: Vintage Books, 1963.

————. *Toward a Theory of Instruction.* Cambridge, Mass.: Belknap Press of Harvard University Press, 1966.

Bruner, Jerome S. and others. *Studies in Cognitive Growth.* New York: John Wiley and Sons, 1966.

Carroll, John B. "Words, Meanings and Concepts." *Harvard Educational Review,* 34, 178–202, Spring 1964.

Cartledge, Connie J. and Edwin L. Krauser. "Training First-grade Children in Creative Thinking under Quantitative and Qualitative Motivation." *Journal of Educational Psychology,* 54, 295–299, December 1963.

Chukovsky, Kornei. *From Two to Five.* Translated and edited by Miriam Morton. Berkeley, Calif.: University of California Press, 1966.

Culkin, John M. "A Schoolman's Guide to Marshall McLuhan." *Saturday Review,* 50, 51–53, 70–72, March 18, 1967.

Deutsch, Cynthia P. and Martin Deutsch. "Brief Reflections on the Theory of Early Childhood Enrichment Programs." Prepared for the Social Science Research Council Conference on Early Childhood Education, Chicago, Illinois: February 7, 8, and 9, 1966. New York: Department of Psychiatry, New York Medical College, Institute for Developmental Studies, 1966. Mimeographed.

Ellis, Richard R. "Educational Programing for Preschool Children." Paper presented at the 44th Annual Convention of the Council for Exceptional Children, April 22, 1966, Toronto, Canada. New York: Department of Psychiatry, New York Medical College, Institute for Developmental Studies, 1966. Mimeographed.

————. "Innovations in the Pre-Kindergarten Program." Paper presented at the Institute for Developmental Studies Workshop-Conference, June 6, 1966, held for administrators and supervisors from District 6M. New York: Department of Psychiatry, New York Medical College, Institute for Developmental Studies, 1966. Mimeographed.

Falcone, Mae Victoria. "Artistic Experiences for Children: Their Significance in Elementary Education." Doctor of Education Project Report. New York: Teachers College, Columbia University, 1961. Typewritten.

Finney, Ross Lee. "Analysis and the Creative Process." *Scripps College Bulletin,* 2, 1–17, February 1959.

Fowler, Charles B. "Discovery Method: Its Relevance for Music Education." *Journal of Research in Music Education,* 14, 126–134, Summer 1966.

Friedenberg, Edgar Z. "Recess." *New York Review of Books,* 6, 21–22, July 7, 1966.

Friedlander, Bernard Z. "A Psychologist's Second Thoughts on Concepts, Curiosity, and Discovery in Teaching and Learning." *Harvard Educational Review,* 35, 18–38, Winter 1965.

Fromberg, Doris P. "The Reactions of Kindergarten Children to Intellectual Challenge." Doctor of Education Project Report. New York: Teachers College, Columbia University, 1964. Typewritten.

Fromm, Erich. "The Creative Attitude." Harold H. Anderson, ed. *Creativity and Its Cultivation.* New York: Harper & Row, 1959, pp. 44–54.

Gagne, Robert M. *The Conditions of Learning.* New York: Holt, Rinehart and Winston, 1966.

————. "The Learning of Concepts." *The School Review,* 73, 187–196, Autumn 1965.

Gallagher, James J. *Teaching the Gifted Child.* Boston, Mass.: Allyn and Bacon, 1964.

———. *Trends and Needs in Educating the Gifted: A Critique.* U.S. Office of Education, OE-35056, Bulletin 1965, no. 6. Washington, D.C.: Government Printing Office, 1965.

Gibson, Eleanor J. and Vivian Olum. "Experimental Methods of Studying Perception in Children." P. H. Mussen, ed. *Handbook of Research Methods in Child Development.* New York: John Wiley and Sons, 1960, pp. 311–373.

Gray, Susan W. *et al. Before First Grade.* The Early Training Project for Culturally Disadvantaged Children. New York: Teachers College Press, 1966.

Guilford, J. P. "Creative Abilities in the Arts." *Psychological Review,* 64, 110–118, March 1957.

Guilford, J. P. and P. R. Merrifield. "The Structure of Intellect Model: Its Uses and Implications." Psychology Laboratory Report no. 24. Los Angeles, Calif.: University of Southern California, April 1960.

Hallman, Ralph J. "Can Creativity Be Taught?" *Educational Theory,* 14, 15–23, January 1964.

Hamlon, Ruth, Rose Mukerji and Margaret Yonemura. *Schools for Young Disadvantaged Children,* New York: Teacher's College Press, 1967.

Hanslick, Edward. *The Beautiful in Music.* Gustave Cohen, tr. New York: Liberal Arts Press, 1957.

Hechinger, Fred M., ed. *Pre-School Education Today: New Approaches to Teaching Three-, Four-, and Five-Year-Olds.* New York: Doubleday, 1966.

Held, Richard. *Plasticity in Sensory-Motor Systems.* San Francisco, W. H. Freeman, 1961. Reprinted from *Scientific American,* 213, 84–94, November 1965.

Hendrix, Gertrude. "Learning by Discovery: An Analysis of Some Methods of Teaching, Considering the Question, 'What Is the Discovery Method of Teaching.' " *Mathematics Teacher,* 54, 290–299, May 1961.

Hilgard, Ernest R. and Gordon H. Bower. *Theories of Learning.* Third Edition. New York: Appleton-Century-Crofts, 1966.

Holt, John. *How Children Fail.* Delta Book. New York: Dell, 1964.

Huebner, Dwayne, ed. *A Reassessment of the Curriculum.* New York: Bureau of Publications, Teachers College, Columbia University, 1964.

Hunt, Joseph McV. *Intelligence and Experience.* New York: Ronald Press, 1961.

Institute of Developmental Studies. "Proceedings of a Presentation to the Division of Early Childhood and Elementary Education, November 28, 1966." New York: School of Education, New York University, 1966.

Jaques-Dalcroze, Émile. *Rhythm, Music and Education*. Translated from the French by Harold F. Rubinstein. New York: G. P. Putnam's Sons, 1921.

Jersild, Arthur and Sylvia Beinstock. *Development of Rhythm in Young Children*. New York: Bureau of Publications, Teachers College, Columbia University, 1935.

Kagan, Jerome. "Personality and the Learning Process." *Daedalus: Creativity and Learning*, 94, 553-563, Summer 1965.

Kliebard, Herbert M. "Structure of the Disciplines as an Educational Slogan." *Teachers College Record*, 66, 598-603, April 1965.

Lang, Paul Henry. *Music in Western Civilization*. New York: W. W. Norton, 1941.

Langer, Susanne. "The Primary Illusions and the Great Orders of Art." *Hudson Review*, 3, 219-233, Summer 1950.

Leonhard, Charles. "The Next Ten Years in Music Education." *Council for Research in Music Education Bulletin*, no. 7: 13-23, Spring 1966.

————. "The Philosophy of Music Education—Present and Future." *Comprehensive Musicianship*. A report of the Seminar sponsored by the Contemporary Music Project at Northwestern University, April 1965. Washington, Music Educators National Conference, 1965, pp. 42-49.

Lewin, Kurt. *A Dynamic Theory of Personality*. New York: McGraw-Hill, 1935.

Lieberman, Josefa N. "Playfulness and Divergent Thinking: An Investigation of Their Relationship at the Kindergarten Level." Ph.D. Dissertation. New York: Teachers College, Columbia University, 1964. Typewritten.

McLuhan, Marshall. *Understanding Media: The Extensions of Man*. First Paperback Edition. New York: McGraw-Hill, 1965.

Machlis, Joseph. *The Enjoyment of Music: An Introduction to Perceptive Listening*. Revised Edition. New York: W. W. Norton, 1963.

Marshall, Sybil. *An Experiment in Education*. First Paperback Edition. Cambridge: Cambridge University Press, 1966.

Martin, Frank. "La Rythmique Jaques-Dalcroze." *Le Rythme*, October-December, 1955, pp. 3-10.

Mearns, Hughes. *Creative Power: The Education of Youth in the Creative Arts*. Second Edition. New York: Dover Publications, 1958.

Miel, Alice, ed. *Creativity in Teaching: Invitation and Instances*. Belmont, California: Wadsworth Publishing, 1961.

Montessori, Maria. *Dr. Montessori's Own Handbook*. Cambridge, Mass.: Robert Bentley, 1964.

Moorhead, Gladys E. and Donald Pond. *Music of Young Children: I. Chant.* Santa Barbara, California: Pillsbury Foundation for Advancement of Music Education, 1941.

———. *Music of Young Children: II. General Observations.* Santa Barbara, California: Pillsbury Foundation for Advancement of Music Education, 1942.

———. *Music of Young Children: III. Musical Notation.* Santa Barbara, California: Pillsbury Foundation for Advancement of Music Education, 1944.

Moorhead, Gladys E., Florence Sandvik, and Don Wight. *Music of Young Children: IV. Free Use of Instruments for Musical Growth.* Santa Barbara, California: Pillsbury Foundation for Advancement of Music Education, 1951.

Murphy, Gardner. *Freeing Intelligence Through Teaching: A Dialectic of the Rational and the Personal.* New York: Harper & Row, 1961.

Mursell, James L. *Education for Musical Growth.* Boston, Mass.: Ginn, 1948.

———. *The Psychology of Music.* New York: W. W. Norton, 1937.

———. "Growth Processes in Music Education," *Basic Concepts in Music Education,* National Society for the Study of Education, 57th Yearbook, Part 1, Chicago, Ill.: University of Chicago Press, 1958, pp. 140–162.

Music Educators National Conference. *Changing Emphases in Elementary School Music.* Gladys Tipton, ed. Philadelphia, Pa.: The Conference, 1964.

National Education Association. *Productive Thinking in Education.* Mary Jane Aschner and Charles E. Bish, eds. Washington: The Association, 1965.

National Society for the Study of Education. *Basic Concepts in Music Education.* 57th Yearbook, Part I. Nelson B. Henry, ed. Chicago, Ill.: University of Chicago Press, 1958.

Neisser, Ulric. "Cultural and Cognitive Discontinuity." *Anthropology and Human Behavior.* Washington: The Anthropological Society, 1962, pp. 54–71.

New York City. Board of Education. *Pre-Kindergarten Curriculum Guide.* Curriculum Bulletin, 1965–1966 Series, no. 11.

Persichetti, Vincent. *Twentieth Century Harmony.* New York: W. W. Norton, 1961.

Phenix, Philip. "Key Concepts and the Crisis in Learning." *Teachers College Record,* **58,** 137–143, December 1956.

Reichel, Bernard. "Improvisation and the Teaching of Eurythmics." *Le Rythme,* December 1962.

Reimer, Bennett. "The Development of Aesthetic Sensitivity." *Music Educators Journal,* **51,** 33–36, January 1965.

———. "Information Theory and the Analysis of Musical Meaning." *Council for Research in Music Education Bulletin,* no. 2: 14–22, Winter 1964.

Robison, Helen F. "Learning Economic Concepts in the Kindergarten." Doctor of Education Project Report. New York: Teachers College, Columbia University, 1963. Typewritten.

Robison, Helen F. and Bernard Spodek. *New Directions in the Kindergarten.* New York: Teachers College Press, 1965.

Sacher, Jack, ed. *Music A to Z.* New York: Grosset and Dunlap, 1963.

Sanchez, Marta. "Report on the Dalcroze Eurythmics Program at the Pre-Primary Level in the Pittsburgh Public Schools." Interlochen, Michigan: Pan-American Dalcroze Teachers Congress, September 1, 1966.

Sessions, Roger. *The Musical Experience of Composer, Performer, Listener.* New York: Atheneum, 1965.

Shapero, Harold. "The Musical Mind." Brewster Ghiselin, ed. *The Creative Process.* New York: Mentor Books, 1955, pp. 49–54.

Sheehy, Emma D. *Children Discover Music and Dance.* New York: Teachers College Press, 1968.

Smith, Robert Clifford. "Esthetic Theory and the Appraisal of Practices in Music Education." Doctor of Education Thesis. Urbana, University of Illinois: 1964.

Spodek, Bernard. "Developing Social Science Concepts in the Kindergarten." Doctor of Education Project Report. New York: Teachers College, Columbia University, 1962. Typewritten.

Taylor, Calvin W. "Educational Changes Needed to Develop Creative Thinking," National Education Association, *Productive Thinking in Education,* Mary Jane Aschner and Charles E. Bish, eds., Washington: The Association, 1965, pp. 245–269.

Taylor, Harold. "Music as a Source of Knowledge." *Music Educators Journal,* 51, 35–38, 151–154, September–October 1964.

Tipton, Gladys and Eleanor Tipton. *Teacher's Guides for Adventures in Music.* A New Record Library for Elementary Schools. New York, RCA Victor, 1961. Ten Volumes.

Torrance, E. Paul. *Guiding Creative Talent.* Englewood Cliffs, N.J.: Prentice-Hall, 1962.

————. "Scientific Views of Creativity and Factors Affecting Its Growth." *Daedalus: Creativity and Learning,* 94, 553–563, Summer 1965.

Trotter, Robert. "On the Teaching of Musicianship in Today's Schools from Kindergarten through the Doctorate." Address, Seventh Biennial Conference, August 22–26, 1966. Interlochen, Michigan, International Society for Music Education, 1966. Mimeographed.

U.S. Office of Education. *Learning about Learning.* Jerome S. Bruner, ed. OE-

12019, Cooperative Research Monograph no. 15. Washington: Government Printing Office, 1966.

———. *Music in Our Schools: A Search for Improvement.* Report of the Yale Seminar on Music Education. Claude V. Palisca, ed. OE-33033, Bulletin 1964, no. 28. Washington: Government Printing Office, 1964.

Varese, Edgar. Taped interview of Edgar Varese by Eric Salzman. Rebroadcast, WBAI, New York City, November 30, 1966.

Wallach, Michael A. "Art, Science, and Representation: Toward an Experimental Psychology of Aesthetics." Robert J. C. Harper and others, eds. *The Cognitive Processes.* Englewood Cliffs, N.J.: Prentice-Hall, 1964, pp. 412–426.

———. "Research on Children's Thinking." National Society for the Study of Education. *Child Psychology.* 62nd Yearbook, Part I. Harold Stevenson, ed. Chicago, Ill.: University of Chicago Press, 1963, pp. 236–276.

Wann, Kenneth D., Miriam Selchen Dorn and Elizabeth Ann Liddle. *Fostering Intellectual Development in Young Children.* Foreword by Alice Miel. New York: Teachers College Press, 1962.

KINDERGARTEN MUSIC TEXTS

Berg, Richard C. *et al. Music for Young Americans: Sharing Music.* Kindergarten. Second Edition. New York: American Book, 1966.

Boardman, Eunice and Beth Landis. *Exploring Music: Kindergarten.* New York: Holt, Rinehart and Winston, 1969.

Grentzer, Rose Marie and Marguerite V. Hood. *Birchard Music Series: Kindergarten.* Evanston, Illinois: Summy-Birchard, 1959.

Jaye, Mary Tinnin and Imogene Hilyard. *Making Music Your Own.* Kindergarten. Morristown, New Jersey: Silver Burdett, 1966.

McCall, Adeline. *This is Music.* Kindergarten and Nursery School. Boston, Mass.: Allyn and Bacon, 1965.

Smith, Robert and Charles Leonhard. *Discovering Music Together: Early Childhood.* Chicago: Follett, 1968.

Watters, Lorrain E. *et al. The Magic of Music.* Kindergarten. Boston, Mass.: Ginn, 1965.

Wilson, Harry R. *et al. Growing with Music.* Kindergarten. Englewood Cliffs, N.J.: Prentice-Hall, 1966.

CHILDREN'S BOOKS

Borton, Helen. *Do You Hear What I Hear?* New York: Abelard-Schuman, 1960.

deRegniers, Beatrice Schenk. *The Shadow Book.* New York: Harcourt, Brace & World, 1960.

Fait, Gladene Hansen and Hollis F. Fait. *We Do As the Animals Do.* Minneapolis, Minn.: T. S. Denison, 1962.

Fischer, Hans. *Pitschi.* New York: Harcourt, Brace & World, 1953.

Kessler, Ethel and Leonard Kessler. *Big Red Bus.* New York: Doubleday, 1957.

Lenski, Lois. *Cowboy Small—Vaquero Pequeno.* New York: Henry Z. Walck, 1960.

————. *The Little Train.* New York: Henry Z. Walck, 1940.

MacDonald, Golden and Leonard Weisgard. *Whistle for the Train.* New York: Doubleday, 1956.

Reid, Alastair. *Ounce Dice Trice.* Boston, Mass.: Little, Brown, 1958.

Slobodkina, Esphyr. *Caps for Sale.* New York: William R. Scott, 1960.

Tresselt, Alvin. *White Snow, Bright Snow.* New York: Lothrop, Lee and Shepard, 1947.

INDEX

Items in the Appendix are included

Displacement, 20
Divided beat
  experience involving, 110
  game involving, 55
Drum, 50, 79
Durations, patterns of, 57
Dynamics, 24, 43, 98, 117, 159
  changing, 100, 107, 125

E

Echo game, 78
  high-low, 86
Education
  defined, 17
  as dual process, 8
Educational goals, comprehensive, 17,
  163
Emotional development (*see* Affective
  development)
Emotionally-disturbed children, 163
Enactive mode (*see* Enactive representation)
Enactive representation, 8, 32, 62
  defined, 7
Enactive-iconic relationship, 35
Energy release through movement
  inventions, 53
Environmental sounds, 85
  teacher's awareness of, 59
Esthetic creation, 16
Esthetic experience
  of composer, 16
  defined, 17
  of listener, 16
  of performer, 16

Esthetic expression, young child's, 20
Esthetic systems, 14
Esthetic theory, 14
  music educator's study of, 14
Esthetics (*see* Concepts *about* music)
Eurythmics, Dalcroze, 165
  defined, 166
  principles, *defined,* 167
  rationale, 168
    verified, 171
  study techniques, 168
Evaluation
  planning, use in, 149
  teacher's observations, 59
Even sounds, less than a beat, 22
Ev'rybody Loves Saturday Night, 120
Exemplar of concept, 30
Experimentation with musical mate-
  rials, 21
Expression, manipulation of elements
  for, 118
Expressive potential of musical elements, 170

F

Finger cymbals, performance tech-
  nique, 84
Finney, Ross Lee, 35
Folk songs, 70
Follow, game, 167
Following the music, 152
Foreign language songs, 70
Form (*see* Design)
Formalists, 16
Fromberg, Doris, 10

G

Gallop, rhythmic pattern, 111
Galloping
  pattern on rhythm sticks, 51
  against triplets, 119
Games
  child leading, 55
  high-low, 86
  song repertoire, 134
  teacher supplying music, 54
  traditional, 63
  uses of, 54
Getting faster (*see* Agogics)
Getting softer (*see* Decrescendo)
Guides, teacher, use of, 59

H

Hanslick, Edward, 15
Held, Richard, 171
High Life, 121
High-low, 73, 85, 117, 154
Hiney Matov
  Complete, 98
  Part A, 88
Hopping, 101
Hot Cross Buns, 124
  notation of, 145
Human experience of music, 34
Hunt, Joseph McV., 6

I

Iconic mode (*see* Iconic representation)

Iconic representation, 8, 32, 62
  defined, 7
Imagery, kinesthetic, 98
Imagination, young child's, 19
Imitation, teaching by, 31
Improvisation
  piano, limitations of, 61
  teacher's
    on classroom instruments, 61
    for movement, 61
  vocal
    advantages of, 61
    use during other activities, 62
Improvising
  objectives of, 151
  rhythmic patterns, clapping, 158
  words to melody, 129
Instrumental accompaniment, child's, 161
Instruments, tone quality of, 24
Intellectual development, modes of, 7
Intelligence, 3
  defined, 7
  growth rate, 5
Interaction of modes, 33
Interrupted canon, 75
  game, 167
Introduction, "orchestral," 130
Inventions, movement, 53

J

Jaques-Dalcroze, Émile, 8, 29, 34
  contribution to music education, 166
  educational objectives, 170

Note values, 145

O

Objectives
  long range, 149
  samples of, 149
Observation
  checklist of affective behavior, 150
  teacher's evaluation of demonstra-
    tions, workshops, 59
Orchestration, 56
Orff, Carl, 29
Orienting to space, 70

P

Patterns, melodic (*see* Melodic pat-
    terns)
Patterns, rhythmic (*see* Rhythmic pat-
    terns)
Perception
  characteristic of young child's, 19
  as cognition, 17
  in music learning, 18
Perception and response, Dalcroze's
    rationale, 170
Performance (*see* Skills)
Performance skill
  jingle bells, 106
  piano, 123, 124
Performance technique, piano, 95
Phenix, Philip, 9
Philosophy
  as guide for teaching, 41
  of music education, 13

Phrase, analysis of expressive potential,
    170
Phrasing, 116, 161, 169
  repetition of words, 132
Piaget, Jean
  contributions of, 7
  limitations of theories, 10
Piano, 52
  for analyzing melodic shape,
    138
  high-low, 87
Pitch, 23
Pitch levels
  high-low, 108
    game involving, 55
Planning music-movement session,
    66
Plastique animé, 170
Playing
  as extension of body movement, 45
  objectives, 151
  use in discipline, 63
Playing for movement
  beat, 154
  meter, 154
Polymeter, 169
Polyrhythm, 169
Practical order of presentation, 66
Practice, relation to research, 163
Prelearning, 7
Preverbal intelligence, conditions for
    transfer, 6
Principles (*see* Concepts, chain of)
Prose
  rhythm, 23, 117
  singing, 126

Q

Quick response, 152
  aspect of games, 54
  games, 80, 81, 110, 114, 167
  rhythmic patterns, 101

R

Range, singing, 152
Rationale, 3, 13, 41, 163
  Jaques-Dalcroze's, 171
  need for, 12
Raw sounds, 24
  teacher's experimentation with, 59
Reading, an skill, 25
Reafference, 62, 89, 115, 171
  defined, 171
Records
  limitations of use, 61
  use during other activities, 65
  use for movement, 61
Registers, contrasting, on piano, 125
Reimer, Bennett, 16, 18
Repertoire, 161
  for concept formation, 30
  defined, 18
  patterns and qualities of sound, 25
Repetition, 25
Representation, *defined,* 32
Research, relation to practice, 163
Response
  as affection, 16
  in music learning, 18
Rests, 23, 168
  at beginning of measure, 120

introduction of, 78
Rhythm, 22, 42
  defined, 34
Rhythm instruments, traditional use of, 44
Rhythm sticks, 51
Rhythmic patterns, 23, 81, 126, 153
  clapping, 155
  stepping, 168
Richard's Song, 128
Rig-a-jig-jig, 118
Ritsch Ratsch, 97
Robison, Helen, 10
Rock Island Line. The, 108
Roll call, singing, 76
Rote memory, 31
Running, 120

S

Sacher, Jack, 15
Scale
  major, 93
  natural minor, 94
  on piano, 95
Science learning, 45
Self expression, 4
Sessions, Roger, 34
Shape, melodic (*see* Melodic shape)
Shape, rhythmic, 23
  See also Rhythmic patterns
Sierra Leone, language of, 121
Silence, in musical expression, 45
Singing, 132
  objectives, 151
  as skill, 25

Tone-matching games, 64
Tone qualities, patterns of, 57
Tone quality, 24, 42, 118, 125
    expressive potential, 45
    game involving, 55
    of instruments, 118
       recognition of, 159
    orchestration, 130
Traditional activities, objectives of, 3
Transformation, 169
Translation of modes, 67, 69
    enactive and iconic, 33, 89, 171
Triangle, 48, 82
    performance technique, 84
       tremolo, 82

U

Uneven beats and measures, 170
Uneven measures, 57

Upbeat (*see* Anacrusis)

V

Varese, Edgar, 34
Verbalizing concepts, objectives, 151
Visual imagery, 7, 66, 115
    from children's book, 71
    from experience, 72
Vocal improvisation, teacher's, 77, 128
Vocal range, adjusting to child's, 76
Voice, 45
Voice control, 132
Voices, tone quality of, 24

W

Wake Me!, 104
Walking, 120
    against divided beat, 119
Wann, Kenneth, 10